SHOPPING IN REGE

Surr's Trade Card

Front cover: Taylors Tea Rooms (next to Kleiser's Court), Stonegate, York. The Mr Kleiser of Kleiser's Court was not a Regency shopkeeper but a Victorian watchmaker.

In everloving memory of

BERKELEY

Cani semper fideli

*Shopping in Regency York:
1811 to 1820*
Butcher, Baker, Candlestick-Maker

Prudence Bebb, BA

Sessions Book Trust
York, England

© Prudence Bebb, 1994

ISBN 1 85072 148 3

The author wishes to express her thanks to Mr I. E. Reynolds of Stephenson and Son for allowing her to view William Alexander's old premises, at what is now No. 20 Castlegate. She is also very grateful to the staff at the York City Archives and at York Reference Library. Illustrations of trade cards are included courtesy of Richard Stansfield, Castle Museum, York, to whom the author is most grateful and she extends her thanks to Mr Jonathan Wild of Betty's Café Tea Rooms, Harrogate, for permission to use the cover picture. She is also indebted to her mother, Elsie Bebb, for assistance with the Index.

Thomas Chapman's Trade Card

Printed in 10 on 11 point Bembo Typeface
by William Sessions Limited
The Ebor Press, York, England
Successors to William Alexander of Castlegate, York

Contents

Chapter		Page
I	Windows and Wares	1
II	Perfume and Pomatum	8
III	Comfort or Corsets?	14
IV	Tin Plate and Teapots	19
V	Harness and Hoofs	23
VI	Sarsenet and Superfine	30
VII	Bread and Brawn	34
VIII	Reading and Remedies	42
IX	Hats and Hose	49
X	Crispin's Craftsmen	53
XI	Assistants and Apprentices	58
XII	Medicine Men	64
XIII	Chairs and Chattels	70
XIV	Gleam of Gold	76
XV	Who Was Where?	80
	Bibliography	82

Illustrations

	Page		Page
Surr's Trade Card	i	Home of the Tukes in Castlegate	40
Thomas Chapman's Trade Card	iv	Ann Alexander's pamphlet	41
Shop where Mrs Lyon sold corsets	2	Window in Alexander's House	42
Stonegate shop, typically Georgian	2	Curved wall in Alexander's House	43
Shop about 1814 in Ousegate	5	Staircase in Alexander's House	44
Regency shop front decoration	5	John Wolstenholme's Minerva	45
Shops in Ousegate	6	Bay windows	47
The Glover's Trade Card	7	Ann Alexander's 1817 booklet	48
The embarrassed traveller	10	Bonnet and Spencer	50
Mr Parsons' shop	11	Mr Calvert's boot shop	54
Mr Parsons' rainwater head	12	Shoemakers at work	56
Long stays gave a slim line	14	Hessian boot	57
Shop scene	15	Parcel being delivered	58
Royal corsets	15	The tailor's shop	60
Mrs Lyon's sash windows	16	Apprentice cum delivery boy	61
Stonegate with people shopping	20	Regency shop interior	63
Mr Bearpark's seed shop	21	Mr Palmer's apothecary	65
From a Georgian Cookery Book	22	Jars of remedies in shop window	68
A coach leaving The York Tavern	24	A cabinet-maker	71
Ostler in riding boots	25	A lady on a Roman-style chair	72
Ostler in leather breeches	26	A craftsman turning chair legs	73
Coach beside The Black Swan	28	A highly-valued pianoforte	74
Coach broken down	29	Plasterwork above windows	75
An assistant unrolls fabric	30	Gowned for the evening, 1817	76
Morning dress, 1816	33	Silver token shilling, 1811	79
Regency and Tudor in Ousegate	34	Lady shopping	81
A butcher's in Low Ousegate	36	MAP OF YORK, 1818	86
The baker at work	37		
Grocer's window	38		

I

Windows and Wares

NOT A WIRE TROLLEY to be seen; not a plate glass window in sight. If you went shopping in Regency York, you'd walk down a road of timbered jettied buildings, left over from Tudor times and looking rather crumbly, interspersed with 'modern' brick shops with bow windows. Looking through these windows to see what they'd got for sale, you would have a slight difficulty; the elegant bow was divided into little rectangles by narrow wooden mullions and transoms so that you didn't get a complete picture of the items which were arranged on four shelves. Boots and pies, bonnets and parasols, books and pistols might seem a little odd, distorted by the thick glass, so that it was better to go inside and have a closer look.

You usually climbed a couple of rather steep steps, clutching the iron rail if you needed it, before opening the door and walking up to a high wooden counter.

No tills in here, just wooden drawers with a leather-bound ledger lying on the counter and quill pens in an inkwell made of heavy pewter with a broad base – the kind used by a naval captain and designed not to slither around the desk in heavy seas.

If you bought something which needed weighing, the shopkeeper could use any weights he chose on the balance scales. This might lead to deliberate or accidental mistakes. For example, a 10 and an 11 pound weight would look very similar and so the wrong one might be used. Nowadays, to avoid this chicanery, only certain weights are permitted. It used to be said that each butcher had a heavy thumb but really he didn't need it if he could sneak the wrong weight onto the scales.

If your purchase did indeed weigh heavily, it could be wrapped in brown paper by the assistant at the counter and then the apprentice would be ordered to carry it home for you.

The 20th-century shopper, straying into Regency York, would be confused by the frequent use of the word 'warehouse' and might suppose that the place was full of repositories for wholesale goods. Not so. House may equal home nowadays but then its meaning was more like 'building'. Hence a family home for sale was advertised as a 'dwelling house' and a warehouse was literally a building displaying wares for sale, i.e. a shop.

Shop used in the Regency. Close by Mrs Lyon sold corsets

Stonegate shop, typically Georgian

Most of York's old shops windows have been superseded by plate glass but there are a few left. In Stonegate both those at Taylor's Tea Rooms and at Pitlochry have survived; elsewhere as in Coney Street, the upper floors of the 'warehouses' of Regency days are still there. It's worth straining your neck muscles for a few minutes to gaze up at the rows of sash windows set in narrow bricks; here we have the upstairs windows of the glovers, drapers, milliners, grocers and booksellers of Regency York. Now replace the ground floor with mental images adapted from Pitlochry and Taylor's and you have a fairly accurate picture of a shopping street in the days when the soldiers from Fulford Barracks marched to face the Eagles of Napoleonic France.

Many shopkeepers were prosperous and could afford to wear the blue-tailed coat so fashionable amongst gentlemen, although the grocer might add a voluminous white apron to protect his pantaloons. Some shopkeepers wore old-fashioned knee-breeches and left their tailed coats open, hanging loosely.

They weren't all wealthy; the newspapers recorded the occasional bankruptcy, a terrible thing in those days when a debtor faced being incarcerated in the county prison with no hope of being free again until his debts were paid. All bankrupts had to give a list of their assets which were promptly sold by commissioners appointed to reimburse the creditors. It was dangerous, if tempting, to refuse to disclose all your assets – in fact, it was labelled a 'felony' and could result in trial with a sentence of transportation. This meant being banished to Australia for a given period but, since your fare home was not paid, it could result in permanent exile, parting a man from his wife, children and friends and thereby punishing them too.

The bankrupt's stock-in-trade might be sent to a different town for sale. In 1815 York people got the chance to buy gold jewellery at knock-down prices in Stonegate when the goods of a bankrupt from another town were auctioned on two successive March days in a shop close to the Star Inn.

However, most of York's shops seemed to deal profitably. It wasn't wise to steal from them. The theft of anything worth more than a shilling was punishable by death. York shopkeepers contributed through the Parish Rate to the wages of a watchman who patrolled the area with staff, lantern and rattle every night.

The shopkeepers themselves had to be cautious not to break laws aimed at protecting the nation's trade. If a haberdasher had gloves, silks or laces from abroad for sale, he or she was really in trouble. A fine of not less than £200 was levied on any draper who had even a pair or two of foreign gloves or a bit of French lace. Our 'Common Market' would have astonished the poor haberdasher who, in January 1811, was mulcted of £300 for this offence and would have put out of business the daring smugglers who frequented the Yorkshire coast.

Shopkeepers could make a 'bit on the side', however, in a perfectly legal way by acting as agents for various diversions. Samuel Knapton and his partner

Mr Erskine at the Music Warehouse in Coney Street sold tickets in February 1812 for a concert with 'singer, pianoforte and oboe' and a Ball to follow. Mr McLean, the boot and shoemaker farther along Coney Street, sold two shilling tickets for Dr Arbuckle's performance 'when he will introduce the most . . . truly astonishing Magical Illusions, ever witnessed here, or in any part of the known world. . . .' One could even buy a national lottery ticket at a bookshop with the possibility of four prizes worth £20,000 – equivalent to a monumental Pools win nowadays.

Outside sounds, such as the cry of the street seller, penetrated the 'warehouse'. Rolling wheels and clopping hoofs announced the arrival of a coach which darkened the shop as the big vehicle passed the small window.

Even shop windows were subject to changes in fashion. The early ones really were semi-circular but in the late 18th century they were flatter with rounded corners like the one still to be seen on the north side of Low Ousegate. By the Regency years a new style was being built – completely flat but still divided by thin bars and often ornamented at the top.

If you wanted your shop to look different from others, you could introduce restrained decoration above the windows and over the doorway. Bunches of bell-flowers or delicate festoons of corn husks were favourites; sometimes the mask of a satyr or the head of a Greek god gave a classical touch to a provincial shop.

Some of these survive. Number 65, Low Petergate, has subdued floral ornament in elegant curves over the remnant of a Georgian bow window and there's an interesting head above the door at the right of Pitlochry.

Regency shopkeepers never put ugly Sale notices in their windows but they did reduce prices to attract custom. Mr Frankland offered silk shawls, rich coloured velvets and frills for edging a fashionable gown at 'unequalled prices'. There was even a sale of 'Gentlemen's Fashionable London Hats' near the Saracen's Head Inn, Stonegate.

Despite the draconian punishments, people did sometimes steal from shops and the owners liked to be prepared. Mr Clementshaw in Fossgate could supply them with a powerful deterrent – his Patent Burglary Pistol. 'This pistol,' he explained, 'may be placed in any corner of a House or Shop in a small wooden box . . . and if any person enters at either door or window, it fires. . . .' Loaded with ball and powder, it was unlikely to be able to distinguish between a cunning thief and an uninvited aunt. It did ring an alarm bell but it shot the intruder simultaneously!

Some shopkeepers joined the York Association for the Prosecution of Felons, Cheats, and etc.' At the Assizes in 1817, Isabella Thirkill was transported for 14 years for her part in the theft of silk handkerchiefs from Messrs Parsons and Blanchard. Property was regarded as sacred in Regency England.

Shop about 1814 in Ousegate

Typical Regency shop front decoration

5

Shops in Ousegate

If you wished to buy a shop in York, there was no Halifax or Abbey National to give you a mortgage. However, if you couldn't raise the whole price, it was sometimes possible to pay part and owe the rest on security of the property.

When a shopkeeper decided to retire, he would announce that he was 'declining business'. The grocer in Thursday Market advertised his shop in 1813: 'The present occupier declining the business in consequence of its not agreeing with his health'. Not perhaps a very felicitous way of recommending his livelihood to a successor!

But some shopkeepers did nearly work themselves to death – and their apprentices too – for many goods were made on the premises. In back rooms, outhouses and upstairs they stitched, hammered, polished and carved. They made chocolate, gloves, harness, mirrors, goose pies and they slaughtered cattle behind the Shambles.

Others boasted that their goods came direct from the most exclusive 'houses' in the capital. By 'houses' they meant, of course, London shops which not only sold retail to their own customers but also wholesale to provincial tradespeople.

Advertisements were usually obsequious paragraphs in the local paper but many tradespeople had a printed card, suitably engraved in a cartouche or embellished with a little *motif* showing the sort of things they sold. The wording was brief.

Mrs Morgan had a simple card but she also sent a gushing paragraph to *The York Herald* when she acquired the new summer styles.

Fashionable Millinery Rooms
MRS MORGAN

Respectfully informs the Ladies of York and its environs, that her Elegant and Fashionable Assortment of Millinery, Dresses &etc. adapted to the present season, will be ready for inspection in the course of next week. Mrs M begs to assure her friends, that as every attention has been paid in selecting the most fashionable articles, she flatters herself they will meet general approbation. An early inspection will be esteemed a favour..

Coney Street, May 18th 1812

Not for these salespeople the glossy pictures of bits of tortured plastic. They bought and sold and chiselled and cut and baked the natural products of the earth. The wheelwright in Jubbergate repaired a strong second-hand waggon; the confectioner in Coney Street made game pies to order and Mr J. Wisker sold wax candles in Spurriergate.

Many of them made a good living like the stationer who never left his shop from dawn to dusk in 40 years. 'By penurious saving he amassed the sum of £4600.' This was left to his daughters – provided that one of them refrained from marrying any one of a list of young men named in her careful father's will!

The Glover's Trade Card

II

Perfume and Pomatum

CONVENIENTLY NEAR to that Mecca of Regency life, the Assembly Rooms, was the shop of Mr Parsons who sold wigs and cut hair. Of course, wigs were not fashionable anymore but bald gentlemen are always with us; Mr Parsons and his rival in trade, William Hands (who was profitably situated exactly opposite the Assembly Rooms), provided for their needs.

J. Parsons really was a terribly useful man – according to his own estimation, at any rate. He could stop your hair falling out, cure you of gout and send you delicately perfumed into the world. As for his Rowland's Macassar Oil, it even promoted the growth of whiskers and eyebrows; no wonder that it was used by the Duke of Sussex and the Spanish Ambassador. How dreadful it would be for His Excellency if King Ferdinand should send him to another country beyond the reach of an oil which 'possesses properties of the most salubrious nature for restoring the hair where it has been BALD for years, preserves it from falling off or turning grey to the latest period of life'. Even the Princess of Wales used it.

Those who wanted to emulate 'the majority of the Nobility throughout the Empire' could purchase Macassar Oil from Mr Parsons in bottles ranging from three shillings and sixpence to one guinea. Almost like today's free gifts, you got with each bottle a booklet about hair and how it would benefit from the Macassar Oil, giving testimonials from 'persons of distinguished consideration'. Mr Parsons advised putting the oil on the scalp immediately after sea bathing, so anyone about to take the Lord Nelson coach for Scarborough would be wise to pack a bottle. The advertisement also described the oil as 'highly worthy the attention of Parents, Proprietors of Schools, etc.' Were the proprietors of schools supposed to produce glossy-curled pupils or could it be that teachers were expected to turn grey and lose their hair?

However that might be, ladies with matrimonial aspirations (or just flirts) might take comfort from the advertisement since 'Ladies, especially find the beneficial effects of this oil, as it gives to the tresses a most beautiful gloss and scent, and when dressed and curled it renders it inexpressibly attracting. . . .'

It also reminds us that British trading ships went considerable distances; this hair oil contained ingredients from trees on the island of Macassar in the East

Indies, presumably brought to the Port of London in John Company ships and purchased there by Rowland & Son of Hatton Gardens, Kirby Street, London, who made it into the oil sold by many shops all over the country including that of our Mr Parsons.

Gentlemen fed up with stropping their razors could buy Holbrook's Renovator from Mr Parsons. It was 'equally efficacious in making razors shave the strongest beard with the thinnest skin as easy and pleasant as the weakest beard'. Red-coated army officers, leaving for the Peninsula, and veterans of Nelson's campaigns, striding the quarter-deck, were all advised to put the Renovator in their luggage. Then the advertisement faced the facts: 'Most Gentlemen know how to strop a razor though few know how to set one upon a hone.' For these the Renovator was an absolute must.

Mr Parsons claimed he could 'astonish anyone' with Holbrook's Renovator. A true benefactor, Mr Parsons, to those valetless gentlemen who hoped to walk down Coney Street with a close shave, although one can't help wondering how many white cravats were blood-spotted in those days of cut-throat razors.

The tax, levied on hair powder to help prosecute the war against France, proved self-defeating; people simply wore their hair unpowdered and wig-makers like William Hands and Mr Parsons couldn't sell hair powder except to the old-fashioned and affluent.

Mr Parsons would wear a white apron to protect his shirt and waistcoat when lathering and cutting. His customer would be fitted temporarily with a horse-shoe-shaped bowl which held the neck and collected the soapy perfumed drips. At least the soap here was always beautifully fragrant.

If you were old-fashioned and could afford the tax on powder, it was still possible to buy a wig from Mr Parsons. This would be pomaded with pig fat, curled on wooden or clay rollers, baked, then powdered by tiny bellows.

Most men didn't admit that they had insufficient hair to flick into the fashionable windblown style of the young men who surrounded the Regent at Carlton House. Luckily Mr Parsons understood their problems; he went to London himself and bought modish hair-pieces for them. On his return he advertised that he had 'selected from the first manufactories an elegant assortment of ornamental hair'. And he didn't mean the first ones he came to; in Regency terms 'first' means best and most up-to-date.

In 1814 he sent for another consignment of false hair and his advertisement inspired confidence: 'Improved Gentlemen's Wigs, made of Natural Hair, warranted not to shrink nor change colour.' Just as well! A wig, which had diminished in washing, would not conceal its owner's pate very safely. A contemporary illustration of the effects of jolting over a rough road in a coach must have created embarrassing fears.

A lurching coach exposed a bald head

Mr Parsons didn't forget the wives and daughters of his clients. He cut their hair in the latest fashions and obtained head-dresses, tortoiseshell combs and enticing perfumes for them. Fortunately he was getting well known in London among the manufacturers and he got the monopoly for selling the latest 'Ladies' Head-dresses, Gentlemen's Crops, Scalps, and etc. being an exact imitation of the hair growing on the head'.

In 1813 he was able to write an advertisement calculated to make the VIPs of York (and those who wished to be so) flock to his shop. 'J. Parsons begs to present his most grateful acknowledgements to the Nobility and Gentry for their continued and increasing patronage and to inform them that he has just returned from London where he has purchased the most extensive and best selected assortment of Hairs, Perfumery, Combs, and etc.' This can't have been such good news for the many comb-manufacturers in York.

If you lived in a village and couldn't readily reach York, Mr Parsons could make a Beau Brummell-style crop or a Jane Austen-style evening hair-do and send it to you. He promised to do it quickly, too.

He became very popular, so much so that his Blake Street shop was cramped and he had to move. He got a bigger establishment which he described as a 'house adjoining the Mansion House'. There he would cut and style hair, sell false hair pieces, arrange combs on high-piled locks and sell exquisitely perfumed soaps. A visit to his new shop was a delight to the nostrils.

Mr Parsons couldn't curl and snip alone. He needed assistants and these he wanted to train himself. In August 1814 he advertised for an apprentice.

By 1815 he was so well established in his new quarters that he could let clients sit in a private room whilst they had their hair trimmed. His premises were obviously large. He'd found the nine rooms in his previous shop inadequate but in his new place he even had room enough to let 'Genteel Family Lodgings'. His old premises in Blake Street he rented out; Mr Parsons 'had arrived' in style.

The defeat of Napoleon at Waterloo on June 18th that year made Continental trade and travel possible again. Since the French were as famous for their perfumes as their fashions, Mr Parsons definitely scored a triumph in 1818 when he went to Paris and brought back, so he said. 'French perfumery of every description, superior to any ever offered for sale in this city before, especially the *Eau de Cologne*.' To this coup he added a large assortment of wigs made from real hair which wouldn't lose their curl in damp weather.

Mr Hands, still opposite the Assembly Rooms, reacted promptly with an advertisement the following week for 'a genuine and unequalled stock of Foreign Perfumes comprising the much admired *Eau de Cologne*, Eaw Aromatic de Mont

Mr Parsons had his shop adjacent to the Mansion House

Pelier, &c.' Not having been in France himself, he was clearly having trouble with his French spelling but he claimed to have such 'Natural Curled hair as to defy competition, and must be seen to be duly appreciated'. He didn't disdain to sell boot blacking at one shilling a bottle but this was probably beneath Mr Parsons' dignity.

Of course, there were people who boiled mutton fat to make candles and soap (tallow chandlers, they were called), but Mr Parsons' wares were in a different class altogether. He was the source of luxurious fragrance and, in 1819, he finally brought Paris to York. M. Delcroix, the French perfumier, whose premises were in Old Bond Street, London, actually advertised in York's press that '. . . he is continually supplying Mr John Parsons of York with his unequalled foreign perfumery, his much admired *Esprit de Lavande aux Mille Fleurs* . . . he has appointed him to sell the . . . *Poudre Unique* For changing Grey or Red Hair to a Light Colour, Brown or Black'.

Now the most elegant Regency lady, in high-crowned bonnet adorned with ostrich feathers, could make her way to the junction of Coney Street with St Helen's Square to buy that final touch of Gallic polish *Poudre Subtil*.

It was impossible for any rival to compete on even terms with a man who had a monopoly of the sale of exclusive French perfumes. The fashion-conscious flocked to Mr Parsons, until his assistant began to be rude. Mr Parsons was horrified for his clients came from the nobility and Gentry; they weren't the sort to

Rainwater head on Mr Parsons' premises

come back for another toupé or *eau aromatique* if his assistant was going to be cheeky to them; they'd go elsewhere. John Parsons made enquiries and uncovered a plot to rob him of customers which nearly made his own hair stand on end.

He dipped his pen in vitriolic ink and wrote to the newspaper. He was so beside himself that he could no longer apply the rules of English grammar. He began with great dignity in the third person and ended seething with grievance and speaking very personally indeed.

>John Parsons, Ornamental Hair Manufacturer, and Perfumer, Coney-Street, York, is in immediate want of an Assistant.
>
>At the same time wishes to Caution a certain Individual of the Profession, to beware of again employing any mean underhand measures, to seduce persons in my employ to insult my customers, in prospect of his own advantage.
>
>Should also remind Sir Francis, the Orange Merchant, that he had much better not in future lend his assistance to aid the escape of such a vile and unfaithful a Person as my late assistant, to carry off his ill-gotten goods.
>
>JOHN PARSONS

It must have needed a young man of impeccable references and brave spirit to apply for the former assistant's job.

John Parsons and William Hands were surely the most expensive and élite hairdressers in York but they were not the only ones. Twenty-seven of the men who voted in the 1818 General Election gave their occupation as 'hairdresser' but they can't have found it so lucrative as Mr Parsons did. In fact, Christopher Waud, the hairdresser in Thursday Market, added to his income by selling oysters. Some were barbers as well as hairdressers and most of them were working in narrow streets like Francis Spencer, who cut hair in Jubbergate.

They would be glad that the long powdered hair, tied with a bow in the nape of the neck, had finally gone out of fashion. In Italy, Roman remains had been uncovered and the ancient coins showed Caesar with short cropped hair. This had set a fashion which needed careful attention; History had come to the aid of hairdressers.

Today, if you stand on the corner of St Helen's Square and Coney Street appropriately near the perfume shop, you can look across to the store which adjoins the Mansion House and, craning your neck, see its upper storey. There are the sash windows of the top floor of Mr Parsons' premises. You can even see the date 1773 on his rainwater head, proving the building was not new when he moved into it. Here, with French finesse, he perfumed and pomaded the Nobility and Gentry of Yorkshire when they came for Race Week; here too a 'genteel family' might lodge in aromatic and fashionable quarters. Next time you cross the bottom of Coney Street remember Mr Parsons and his scissors.

III

Comfort or Corsets?

A REAL 'slip of a girl' looked marvellous in the classical lines copied from ancient vases dug up in Italy; her mother might not be so fortunate.

Regency fashions were not kind to large ladies. The high waist and tubular skirt flattered the slim and could disguise a thick waist but it was possible to look like one of the miller's sacks of floor, squeezed and bulging. The only hope was the use of 'stays', a type of corset designed to lift the bust and flatten the middle. Putting it on was the problem; unless it was firmly laced at the back, it couldn't function satisfactorily. Mother, husband, sister, dresser – someone was needed to put a foot or knee into the small of the back and pull tightly on the laces.

There were Long Stays which kept madam somewhat rigid as they raised her bosom, held in her stomach and reached to her hips. Made of buckram, with a bone or steel stiffening at the back, they could be tailored to the individual. Uncomfortable certainly, but appearances had to be kept up.

Besides this long version, there were also Short Stays which looked rather like Cinderella's laced bodice but the aim wasn't to look like a European peasant; a lady of classical Greece was the ideal.

Fortunately for the fat, York had a number of shops where stays could be purchased.

Mrs Cooper in Minster Yard described herself as a 'long stay and corset maker'. She said that Minster Yard was a desirable location for business but she and her husband left it two years later and went

Long stays gave a slim line for high-waisted gowns

Mrs Hopton, the stay-maker; Todds the booksellers and Palmer apothecary

to live in Hull. York ladies were told that they could still get their corsets made by Mrs Cooper if they posted their old stays to her at 30 Whitefriargate, Hull.

The removal of Mrs Cooper to Hull was palliated by the continuing work of Mrs Hopton whose workroom and shop were in High Petergate not far from St Michael-le-Belfrey. She could turn out stylishly shaped ladies because she got the latest shapes from London. In January 1814 her advertisement said 'that she has just received a variety of fashionable stays for the present season, among which is the Grecian Bosom'. She could also supply 'Patent Elastic, and Circular Steel Busks of the best quality'. She even had 'An assortment of Servants' Stays at very low prices'. In 1816 she moved and settled next door to Todd's bookshop in Stonegate.

Mr Brown, who was another corset maker, moved *from* his premises in

In 1812 people laughed at the Prince Regent because he needed corsets

15

Stonegate to a shop opposite the dispensary in St Andrewgate. He put a notice in the local paper to let his customers know where he was and took the opportunity 'to return thanks to the Ladies and Others for past favours,' a more innocent phrase than it sounds. The Others were almost certainly the corpulent gentlemen of York who required either to eat less (which was unthinkable) or to get Mr Brown to make them a Cumberland Corset, a whalebone affair which kept the Prince Regent's flabby stomach under some control. The difficulty was that it had a reputation for creaking and one gallant, bending to retrieve a glove for a lady, had the embarrassment of hearing the whalebone snap.

Mr Brown advertised, 'From experience and a thorough knowledge of his Business, he trusts he may please all those who may honour him with their commands'. Then, as if suddenly aware of the delicacy of the situation, he added a postscript to his advertisement: 'Those Ladies who may prefer giving their Orders to one of their own Sex, can be waited on by Mrs B.'

Perhaps the gentlemen might not want to encounter Mrs B; they could always visit Henry Stephenson who sold stays in his Coney Street shop.

There was money in stays. Mrs Lyon, who made corsets for sale in High Petergate, got so many orders she couldn't keep up with them. There was only one thing to be done and she did it in September 1813; she bought a lot of modish stays in London and decided to keep some ready-to-wear on the premises

Mrs Lyon's sash windows

16

to avoid panic and disappointment in future. She had to sell them cheaper than her own make – but not as cheap as those intended for children and servants. Even in those days of sharply defined social ranks, one couldn't expect one's servants to go without stays. There was no need to provide them with the best materials, however; and perhaps it wasn't wise to have very shapely maids if there were gentlemen in the house.

In February 1816 Mrs Lyon was able to announce that she had just received from London some of the latest patterns 'which will be found to fit with ease to the wearer and elegance to the shape'. She was still making them herself and advertised for an apprentice.

'The ladies of York and its Vicinity', so frequently addressed in the newspaper advertisements, could quite literally rely on the shopkeepers of Stonegate for support – especially when Mrs Lyon followed Mrs Hopton into that road. She set up shop opposite to Todds, the booksellers, where she started to sell the latest thing in corsets: 'Elastic French Steel Busks'. Husbands of the brave ladies, who went for fittings, could browse opposite among the various titles at Messrs Todds – but more of them anon.

Mrs Lyon also offered to let 'genteel lodgings' and she was in a good position to do so. Her premises comprised a sizeable Georgian building whose upstairs is still visible above shop level. Her lodgers would have well-proportioned rooms with neat little fireplaces. They also had a view towards the gables and jetties opposite and the sash windows of Mrs Hopton's premises. They would often hear the clopping hooves and female voices which indicated the arrival of another customer and more work for the little apprentice who was learning to stitch hard buckram and insert lengths of whalebone. It was people like Mesdames Hopton and Lyon who kept the whalebone cutters of Hull in business. The modern Regency Miss who refused to emulate her mother's tortured figure (and didn't need to do so) was a disappointment to the Trade. Unfortunately this didn't help the Arctic whales; other uses were found for their bones.

Sometimes London came to York and probably took custom away from the local shops. A certain Mrs Kelsall, 'Corset-maker to Her Royal Highness the Princess Elizabeth' spent a month in April 1815 in Castlegate. It wasn't her first visit to the town and ladies from outlying villages had come previously to sample what she called her 'strict attention united with a general wish of obliging'. Her customers could call on Tuesdays, Thursdays and Saturdays; on the intervening days she was willing to take her tape measure to people in their own homes.

She was back in York in the February of 1817 when she stayed for a couple of weeks 'at Mr Cook's, Bootham'. It seems unlikely that the corset shops of York would welcome her visits; she was definitely a threat to their trade. It is easy to imagine the status gained by those who bought their corsets from her.

'Of course, I always get my stays from Mrs Kelsall; she makes for Princess Elizabeth, you know.' Then, with a pitying glance, 'Who makes *your* stays, dear?'

However, Mrs Lyon was the ultimate beneficiary for, when the Princess's stay-maker died, Mrs Lyon acquired her patterns and was able to offer the Ladies of York and its Vicinity a truly royal uplift.

But Mrs Lyon was to have competition. The peripatetic corset making was not over yet nor was Mrs Kelsall's influence. A lady called Hays, who described herself as 'Successor to the late Mrs Kelsall', went to stay in Scarborough and from there sent notice that she would be coming to York in March and that she had been Mrs Kelsall's assistant for 17 years. So the ladies of York could still imitate the royal shape.

Meanwhile Mrs Hopton advertised for two more apprentices and went to stay in Scarborough herself for a while, assuring her customers that she could fit them with 'equal elegance and taste' to that of Mrs Kelsall.

A month later Princess Elizabeth got married to His Serene Highness Prince Philip Augustus Frederick of Hesse-Hombourg and *The York Herald* obligingly described her going-away outfit – a white satin pelisse (doubtless hanging beautifully over a well shaped figure) and, rather strangely a 'nun's veil', not to be taken too literally for veils of some length were fashionable and could be bought from Mr Welbank the linen-draper in York. It is, of course, possible that the princess intended a little irony. She was 48 and, like her sisters, had been kept by her parents from the society of most men except her brothers to whom the princesses used to write letters headed 'From the Nunnery'.

If you want to see where the larger ladies of Regency York were fitted for their stays, go down Stonegate until you reach the tall jettied building with a square bay window and the Sign of the Bible. This was Todds' bookshop and next door (on the Minster side) is a modern shop front with Georgian sash windows above it. These windows belonged to Mrs Hopton's premises. Opposite to this is the pure Georgian bow window of Taylors' Tea Rooms. Above the present coffee counter and over the shop on the left are more sash windows. Some of them belonged to Mrs Lyon. She and another shopkeeper were·both described as being 'opposite' to the Todds' bookshop so it's difficult to be sure whether she occupied the present Taylor's or its next door neighbour's. However, it is certain that, as you stand beside the tea rooms, you are very close to the workroom where Mrs Lyon's apprentice, with sore fingers, plunged her needle into hard buckram making a Grecian Bosom for a plump English lady.

IV

Tin Plate and Teapots

YOU MIGHT call Mr Pomfret the Mulberry Hall of Regency times. Not only did he respectfully inform the Nobility and Gentry that he had a 'general assortment of Wedgwood's and Spode's Ware of all kinds' but he had it in Stonegate.

It was difficult to compete with Mr Pomfret when he sold Burnished Gold. However, Daniel Knowles, who was entitled the 'Chinaman' of Coney Street, claimed to have the patronage 'of many of the first families in the County'. Beat that, if you can, Mr Pomfret!

He could. He hired the spacious room at the Free Mason's Lodge and exhibited 'the newest and most superb collection' of bronze, crystal, porcelain, coral and shells. He even had among his customers 'Ladies and Gentlemen who have repeatedly applied for bronzed figures' – and this in days when there was no suntan oil! The longed-for statuettes arrived and he set them up on suitable pedestals so they could adorn hallways where they might give the visitor an impression of the elegance, good taste and affluence of the householder, as they were intended to do.

When the war was over, Mr Pomfret was able to import French jars which he unhesitatingly described as 'superior to anything ever seen in this country'.

In 1813 he announced that he had 'a beautiful selection of Fancy Articles' which disappointingly turned out to be lamps and chandeliers. Perhaps a number of customers felt let down for the next year he sold off his lamps cheaply and decided to concentrate on his china and glass.

Mr Pomfret's trading facilities were improved by his connections with Hull. In 1812 he thought of leaving York altogether and simply developing his Hull interests but evidently he changed his mind because he was selling delicate china and strong earthenware in Stonegate several years later. He went into partnership with a Mr Cowley and together they traded from Lowgate in Hull and Stonegate in York. You could get everything from terra cotta to antique china if you visited his showrooms in Stonegate.

He stocked dinner services at prices ranging from five guineas to 55, a vast sum when a kitchen maid was lucky to get £14 a year and the housekeeper only

Stonegate with Regency people shopping

had £24. The same kitchen maid might be expected to crush herbs with a pestle and mortar which Mr Pomfret obtained from the firm of Wedgwood.

He also sold the popular blue and white china which depicted classical ruins and was used on many Regency tables. A tea service might cost from two guineas to five.

Mr Promfret's father (named William like his son) was a Hull man and our William's mother died at Gilberdyke in 1814, the year when Pomfret was described as the sole agent in York and Hull for Liverpool Lamps which he kept in a Hull warehouse, ready packed for export. He had to employ good packers and people who were not too heavy-handed on glass and china, for he sold crystal chandeliers, from which candlelight scintillated, and dainty ornaments intended for the mantlepiece.

Like some of the other shopkeepers he could sell some surprising things. In 1817 he advertised turtles for sale. 'A fine green turtle in excellent condition' might weigh from 30 to 60 pounds. Elizabeth Raffald, in *The Experienced English Housekeeper*, gave detailed instructions on the dressing of a turtle for dinner. When this was being done, she advised: 'Then take out the guts (which are reckoned the best part of the turtle), rip them open, scrape and wash them exceeding well, rub them well with salt, wash them through many waters, and cut them in pieces two inches long. . . .' It was just as well that Mr Pomfret's turtles were no larger for Mrs Raffald said, 'Gravy for a turtle a hundred weight will take two legs of veal and two shanks of beef'.

You would probably require a glass or two of wine with that and Mr Pomfret could supply an elegant wine cooler for it.

This was another example of a shop selling something quite different from its main merchandise. A turtle hardly seems to fit with the bronze candelabra supporting a small waterfall of glass droplets to reflect the candlelight, yet Mr Pomfret sold both.

When his lease on the Free Mason's room ran out, he enlarged his showroom in Stonegate. His 'warehouse' was surely like Aladdin's Cave. He could display the popular cream pottery, French porcelain, oriental jars and china from the Midlands thickly covered with imitation Japanese designs.

Japanned ware of another type would be used in York. Trays of wood or metal were lacquered in black and gold but these were probably obtained from Bilston and elsewhere.

Cook and Son in Colliergate and Benjamin Gorwood in Spurriergate are tantalisingly described as 'tinmen', giving an impression of the toy soldiers popular at the time. Cook and Gorwood both sold items made of tin.

Mr Stodhart, who lived and worked in Coney Street, was also a tinman but he sold items made of brass, copper and wire, too. He made many of the goods in his workshop and could supply vital kitchen equipment like tin lids to cover

Seeds and plants could be purchased from Mr Bearpark whose shop was in this medieval tower

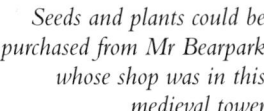

21

dishes of hot food. He sold fire guards, to keep toddlers safe from open coal grates, and Britannia Metal teapots to keep the brew warm. He could make and mend utensils and was probably a busy man. From him you could buy candlesticks, pans, plate-warmers, jelly moulds and even baths.

Most necessary too. Bathrooms were almost unknown but tin tubs and elegant slipper baths were available – one of the French Revolutionary leaders had been murdered in his.

John Stodhart himself died in 1812 and then his house and shop were sold.

People had to go somewhere else for their plate warmers and wire, probably to one of John Stodhart's relations for there was a Thomas Stodhart advertising for an apprentice in 1814 who said he was a wireworker and a 'manufacturer of double block tin and kitchen furniture' – just like John. The furniture wouldn't be chairs or anything like that. In those days furniture meant the contents of the room from door knobs to pans and kettles, which were very likely made by Thomas Stodhart. His block tin would be refined ingots ready for use in his workshop and he probably used some of that to line copper pans. He certainly did repair jobs.

He wasn't the only wireworker. There was Charles Kilvington in the Walmgate area whose descendants now have lovely timbered premises in Stonegate which were three separate households in Regency days.

A neighbour of Charles Kilvington in Walmgate was David Bell, the whitesmith. His trade name tells us that he used non-ferrous metals, unlike the ironmongers and blacksmiths whom we shall meet in another chapter.

Frontispiece from a Georgian Cookery Book 'By a Lady', published in 1809

V

Harness and Hoofs

CREAKING, grinding, trotting, jingling echoed down York's streets; cries of 'Whoa!' and 'Git up there!' pierced the air. Old carts shuddered over cobbles, modern curricles swept round corners and coachmen shouted to ostlers, 'Let 'em go!'

Naturally all this equine activity produced trade; boots, bits and bridles were in constant demand. They didn't need a petrol filling station nor Halfords but they had the Haymarket (where King's Square is now) and the saddlers.

The latter made various kinds of saddles. A side-saddle would be needed for the lady whose habit was made by Hurworths the tailors in Micklegate, its skirt folds elegantly arranged behind her. It wasn't only riders who required saddles; some vehicles, such as curricles, put pressure on the horse's back and a saddle was needed to protect the animal. There was work for about 20 saddlers in a city full of horsemen, coaches and inns.

The prosperity of an innkeeper depended upon the arrival and departure of travellers whose horses were temporarily stabled behind the hostelry. The innkeeper's children could watch innumerable coaches, chariots and gigs carefully negotiating the narrow archway leading to the yard. The coachman on the box seat was a local celebrity holding his jaunty whip at 45 degrees; that sign of his livelihood had probably been made by John Potter, the whip-maker, or Joseph Acomb, his apprentice. There were post boys to watch as well, leaning against the stable wall, bow legs hidden in top boots; the left boot was reinforced to prevent the man's leg being crushed by the nearside horse as he drove the post chaise from his position in the saddle.

An innkeeper's child would grow up surrounded by horses. William Clark's son, George, and Matthew Creaser's son, John, instead of following their fathers' jobs as innkeepers, became fully accredited saddlers – Creaser in 1811, Clark in 1820.

There were two saddlers in Coney Street whilst Micklegate had Hay and Swale, a partnership until Mr Hay decided to go it alone the year of Waterloo.

Mr Spurr, the saddler in Spurriergate, sounds as if he'd strayed into York from a child's card game. In fact, he didn't stay in the business for in 1816 he

A coach leaving The York Tavern, St Helen's Square

was advertising the shop premises with their stock which included glass cases to display the wares and a Saddler's Press.

Some saddlers made other items as well. Mr Pool, whose shop was not far from Mr Spurr's, sold trunks, a useful thing when journeys took days instead of hours, visits lasted weeks and no one had invented a suitcase. Often made of ponyskin, sometimes with a domed lid, the trunk would be strapped to a platform at the back of a post chaise or consigned to the luggage boot of a stage-coach.

Ears pricked intelligently, hoof pawing the ground impatiently, man's assistant from time immemorial was at the mercy of his employer. There were many horse lovers in York but probably just as many people who treated horses as if they were only a means of transport. The RSPCA was badly needed but not started until the next decade. The life of a coach horse was pitifully short. Beaten or made to pull loads too heavy for them, the greys and bays who worked in our city might be very neglected; others were groomed to glossy silkiness and loved as members of the family. All provided trade for various types of shopkeepers.

Ostler in riding boots near the White Horse Inn, Coppergate

Riding boots could be made to measure by Mr Hornby in Stonegate and later by his son. These black boots had a kind of cuff which turned down below the knee revealing the creamy colour of the boot lining.

Walking down the street, it was often possible to see at a glance where to get your equestrian requirements. The bootmaker might display a boot from a hanging sign, especially if he wasn't too bothered by recent legislation which said that only inns should hang signs as a number of unlucky persons had been hit on the head by the crashing of top-heavy signs. The saddler didn't need to hang his advertisement; he simply put a saddle over a wooden support rather like a gymnasium horse. There it stood on the pavement and there wasn't any doubt what he sold.

Leonard Calvert, the bootmaker, only had a small shop in Micklegate and was content to paint his name on a board attached to the jetty between

Ostler in leather breeches beside The White Swan, Goodramgate

his upstairs and downstairs windows. Luckily Henry Cave, a York artist, drew a picture which has preserved Calvert's memory but the actual premises were demolished to make way for Priory Street in more recent times, so we've lost the old priory gateway and Leonard Calvert's little bay window with his boots and shoes arranged for sale.

The saddle-bound posteriors of York wore practical breeches, often made of leather. There was plenty of work for George Allen, the breeches maker in Coney Street, and for Thomas Hardy in Stonegate who, despite his literary sounding name, was another breeches maker.

Besides the saddlers, boot and breeches makers, there were general leather-workers or cordwainers – an old name dating from the days when so much leather came from Cordoba in Spain. One of Regency York's cordwainers had the marvellous name of William Catchasides.

Leather was vital to harness but making harness was a special craft requiring expertise. Broken harness led to accidents.

Although the work of harness and coachmakers was crucial to the safety of travellers, it was important that ostlers coupled and buckled the straps carefully. A careless ostler could create tragedy. Near to Bedford a coach overturned when the pole chain was loose. A contemporary source said, 'One gentleman attempted to jump off; he fell upon his face and the coach fell upon him and on the coachman . . . and when extricated the passenger was quite dead and the coachman severely injured. . . .'

One feels sure that the harness made by Joseph Fisher never left a passenger 'quite dead'. Mr Fisher came from Hull to Ogleforth where he took over the business of Mr Wiseman making both harness and carriages which, he promised, would be 'painted in the most elegant manner and on the most reasonable terms'.

Goods like his were bought directly from the workshops where they were made. When Regency people spoke of a shop, they didn't always mean a building with counters, scales and assistants; they could refer to the blacksmith's forge or the joiner's workshop or the yard where coaches were assembled.

In such a yard Joseph Fisher made any type of carriage to order. This could include phaetons perched high on five foot wheels which were very dangerous and only driven by the intrepid. He was more likely to be asked for the one horse gigs used for local travel; barouches, driven by a coachman and considered suitable conveyances for women and children; which could take families on long journeys; and individual variants of these equipages.

Brearey and Morley sold many kinds of carriage (including second-hand) at their premises which extended from Davygate to Little Stonegate. In 1811

Stage coach outside The Black Swan, Coney Street

they advertised a gig and harness only a year old and London made; they could even provide the horse for it.

That partnership was dissolved and then Brearey took Christopher Myers as his new partner. Morley seems to have set up another firm because in March 1819 there was a business called Morley and Wales (on the corner of Little Stonegate) which was offering for sale a phaeton and second-hand post-chaise. The chaise was a light travelling carriage with only one seat; this faced the horses and the vehicle didn't need a coachman, being driven by a postilion on the offside horse. You changed horses at posting-houses and, when in a hurry, hired four horses – if you could afford them. To buy such a chaise, which was beautifully lined and fitted with red morocco cushions, you needed £40.

Meanwhile Brearey and Myers hoped, they said, to 'receive a continuance of the Favors of the Public, which it will be their constant study to merit by a strict attention to all commands conferred on them'. As an added attraction they had a good hearse for sale.

Next year they advertised for a Coach-Wheeler who had to be a steady workman; he would probably have been trained in a wheelwright's shop where he would have learnt to shape felloes from ash, beech and elm and to pare oak to make spokes no heavier than they needed to be. The loads pulled by horses were quite enough and a skilful coach-wheeler could lighten the load. Mr Brearey's advertisement said, 'None need apply but good workmen'!

The trace of this coach was evidently not fitted by a good workman

VI

Sarsenet and Superfine

DRAPERS WERE WELL NAMED. They draped their blue-spotted muslin, rose-patterned dimity and fine black kerseymere across the doorway. You couldn't have seen what they'd got if they hadn't festooned the open door beneath the fanlight; their bow windows, intersected by slender wooden bars, made a window display of their wares quite impossible. So you climbed the few steps, dodged the hanging fabrics and went inside to look at the black lace and rich silk or the winter fustian and nankeen for boys' trousers.

Bolts of cloth were stacked on shelves to be lifted down and spread over the counter for the customer to feel between finger and thumb the twilled cashmere or glossy lustring.

An assistant unrolls fabric for his customer

The shop would be open until very late in the evening when flickering candles cast the weary assistant's shadow over the cloth which he was measuring in yards, feet and inches. But it wasn't very wise to choose colours in the dim interior. Dark cottons with small flowered *motifs* would be difficult to see. The brown with a tiny rose, the bottle green with a gold bud were hardly distinguishable but ladies seldom shopped after dark. However, gentlemen, critically surveying a coat material of blue superfine, might have the advantage of the shopkeeper's Argand lamp which was as powerful as ten candles but expensive because it used so much oil.

York had two kinds of draper.

The linen-draper sold the lighter fabrics, muslin for high-waisted gowns and silk to wear at the Assembly Rooms. They advertised fashionable 'dresses' but really there was nothing to buy 'Off the Peg'; by 'dresses' they meant the material to make them but their customers understood this.

The woollen-drapers stocked warmer tougher fabrics. John Hodgson, in High Ousegate, was one of the most useful men in York. He had practical commonsense materials which wouldn't easily tear. He even sold Fox's Patent Aquatic Hair Gambroons, just the thing for men who rode over Severus's Hills in the driving rain as G. Fox's Gambroons seem to have been a waterproof heavy-duty fabric which Mr Hodgson advised for collars on driving coats (such as stage-coachmen might use) and for breeches which got frequent rubbing in the saddle.

Some shopkeepers combined linen and woollen drapery but they needed bigger premises with a bow window either side of the entrance and rooms that extended a long way backwards. The present Pitlochry in Stonegate shows us the sort of shop they needed but few could afford to stock it. It was easy for a draper to go bankrupt.

Mr Hewett, whose shop was in Pavement, was quite literally unfortunate.

When the war was spoiling the cotton trade, he bought fabrics at the new cheap prices so he could sell bargains in York. It should have made him rich but it didn't. He went bankrupt and his stock of embroidered muslins, black silk stockings, warm flannel and dainty thread lace were sold at less than cost price. The elderly poor would hobble gratefully into his shop; there were no state pensions and a flannel petticoat was a life-saver when the north wind blew through rotting wattle and daub.

After the war, bargains increased and sometimes special reductions were available for cash sales. Too often shopkeepers were kept waiting for money from customers who deliberately delayed paying their bills.

Price tickets didn't mean so much in Regency times as they do today. The Regency shopper calculated how much he could induce the shopkeeper to reduce the price. The first man to fix immutable prices to his wares was a London bookseller but it was generally thought this wouldn't work; however, it did.

Mr Welbank, a York linen-draper, determined to do the same in 1815. He wouldn't put the highest price he could hope for and let people beat him down; he'd put the lowest price he could afford to take and accept nothing less. His days of haggling were over.

Among the timbered buildings nestling near the Minster, like chicks beside a hen, Mr Welbank had his drapery. Here, in Minster Yard, he sold a thin linen called cambric. However, the most fashion-conscious might not consider him quite up to their standard because his goods came from Manchester and, if they could afford materials from 'the first houses in London', they would go to Bickers and Sowerby in Coney Street.

The less affluent would certainly frequent Mr Welbank's shop. He had plenty of customers, needed an apprentice and finally moved to a shop on a corner site opposite the West Door of the Minster, not that the Minster would be as clearly visible as now. The road leading to it didn't look much like the present Duncombe Place, being narrow and terminating by the great gateway to what was really a Cathedral Close. At this corner Mr Welbank set up his new shop although there's nothing to see of it now. If you are carefully crossing the road diagonally opposite the café, you tread where Mr Welbank sold haberdashery to those who, in his own words 'are pleased to honour him with their support'.

He also wanted them to honour him with cash. Not for him the banknotes from outside York area nor long-dated Bills of Exchange. These bills were issued by bankers and others with resources (sometimes shopkeepers) stating: 'I promise to pay' a specified sum on a particular future date. The bills were circulated as currency when there weren't enough coins during the war. People might pay in shops with them, provided the shopkeeper would accept them. However, bills dated a long time ahead or written by unknown persons were a dubious form of payment. Mr Welbank wouldn't touch anything like that. 'W.W. will conduct his business on Ready Money terms only,' he said. And that was that.

There were more than 40 drapers in York. One of them, Mr Stephenson, had a shop on the site now occupied by Waterstones the booksellers.

The fashion-conscious ladies could turn appropriately to Mrs Peacock who would decorate them from bonnet crown to flounced hem. She deserves a mention in this chapter because she sold haberdashery and materials for baby clothes plus the latest silks and embroidered muslins. Yet she was literally a cut above being a mere draper for, when ladies had chosen their fabrics, she could make them into classical gowns and even provide the latest shape of bonnet which she would trim to match the gown. It was also possible to get alterations done in her Spurriergate shop; she had an apprentice specially set aside for 'improvements', such as letting out bodices to fit the expanding figures of York or adding ribbons of the latest shade to regenerate last year's muslin.

Her materials came from London and her daughters went there to choose them, At the beginning of each season the new cottons, patterns and bonnets arrived from the capital in Spurriergate and she announced, 'Mrs Peacock has

A modish lady in a morning dress made of fashionable London materials in 1816

the honour to inform the Ladies of York and its Vicinity, that her daughters are now returned from London, where they have selected an elegant assortment of millinery, dresses, etc. which will be ready for their approbation . . . when the honour of a call will be gratefully attended to.'

After more than 30 years Mrs Peacock found her large shop getting too much for her so she sold the drapery business and continued making gowns and trimming hats upstairs but at that point she ceased to be a draper and so we will leave her there with her daughters and their assistants and a stock of new bonnets.

VII

Bread and Brawn

'DON'T CRY STINKING FISH!' Maybe not, but it might be an honest description. In the days of no refrigeration, buying sea fish could be a risky business. Our national dish was certainly NOT fish and chips; the cooks of Regency York weren't silly enough to ask for 'Fresh Haddock'. Wooden barrels, packed with ice, were no adequate substitute for sub-zero temperatures. One Regency recipe warned that mackerel 'are so tender that they carry and keep worse than any other'.

Ousegate had Regency buildings on one side with old Tudor shops opposite

No wonder that people ate so much river fish and it's not surprising that fish shops were rare. On Thursdays and Saturdays freshwater fish was sold in St Sampson's Square, then called Thursday Market.

Oysters were cheap and obtainable from some shops which didn't stock any other sort of food. They could be kept alive until required for the table so they were a wise alternative to the highly spiced dishes concocted by some cooks to disguise the flavour of fish which hadn't been in the sea for some time.

There were, of course, many affluent homes in Bootham, Micklegate, Castlegate and St Saviourgate where the kitchen staff observed the injunctions of recipe books to look for thick firm flesh and to remember that 'when flabby they are not good'.

Naturally the butchers did a good trade and there were many of them. Some of them still used medieval premises with a wide wooden window-ledge which doubled as a counter. There are several still existing, including the one at Collectables – a gift shop which still has the hooks where meat hung and a passage where cattle were slaughtered.

The Shambles was still a popular location for butchers. The present Edinburgh Woollen Mill in that street was once called the Eagle and Child but was the home of John Smith, who had a butcher's shop on the ground floor with a parlour behind it and a back entrance from Colliergate.

Housekeepers were urged to buy the meat of animals which had been pastured on short sweet grass in pure air, as the flavour would be better than that from beasts kept in closely confined quarters. Some York butchers grazed their animals outside the city. Thomas Severs kept his sheep in a field near Huntington and this proved a temptation for someone who certainly thought he might as well be hung for a sheep as a lamb. One of the wethers was killed and its carcase taken away. But Mr Severs belonged to the City of York Association for the Prosecution of Felons, Cheats, &c. They offered five guineas to anyone who could give information which would bring the thief to conviction and Severs himself offered to double that.

Henry Cave drew two pictures of a butcher's shop in Low Ousegate in 1813 and here we can see the legs of mutton suspended from meat hooks which haven't changed much to the present day (see p. 36).

One of the shops which had land sloping down to the river was Mr Baker's in Coney Street; here there were outhouses suitable for baking bread or stabling a horse. He sold 'Real Canterbury and Cambridge Brawn' and one could even roost there for William Baker had 'genteel lodgings' to let. On the other hand, if he owed you money you might be unlucky because he went bankrupt in 1811 and John Hearon, the solicitor, called his creditors to a meeting at The Black Swan in Coney Street (on the site of the modern British Home Stores) at 11 in the morning on the 21st of March. There Mr Baker's assets would be shared out.

A butcher's shop in Low Ousegate

Perhaps there was enough to pay all debts because he doesn't seem to have landed in prison. In 1812 he was still selling brawn with a selection of pickles and rich sauces. He took orders for Game and Goose Pies which he promised to dispatch, carefully packed, to 'any part of the kingdom'. Two years later he was celebrating the end of the war against Napoleon – or what everyone hoped was the end; Boney had been defeated and exiled and no one could predict how he would terrify Europe again. William Baker acquired lots of lamps which he loaned to patriotic persons who wanted to place them in their windows. By the time Napoleon was finally defeated in June 1815, William Baker also met his Waterloo. His house and shop were on sale with all the land behind them.

He wasn't the only one who sold Goose and Game Pies; so did Richard Brown in Coney Street and he provided for harassed innkeepers 'on the very lowest terms'. Probably his brawn was put on the 'cold stand' which was a shelf of pies, cold meats and cheeses always available for hungry travellers who hadn't time to wait for a meal to be cooked whilst the horses were changed.

Richard Brown added to his attractions by selling National Lottery tickets to his customers who could add to the excitement of sampling his delicacies by having a little flutter.

Overworked innkeepers might also patronise Mr Elliott, the pastrycook whose shop was near Mr Baker's premises in Spurriergate. Here you could buy sauces which, Mr Elliott said, were perfection. It was, perhaps, wise to check the colour of the sauce before pouring it over the recommended turbot or salmon because Mr Elliott also sold bottles of liquid blacking to give gentlemen's boots a mirror-bright gloss.

However, the 'sauces' and 'catsups' were made in London so Mr Elliott was giving York some of the very first convenience foods. He promoted another modern taste for he sold curry powder 'with a receipt for making a dish after the Indian manner'. But his usefulness did not stop with Essence of Lobsters and Oyster Ketchup. He made pies, specially decorated for Christmas, which he would dispatch to your home.

The baker at work

A baker's shop would comprise stores for corn, an oven set in the wall and heated by the fire, and the actual shop where customers could see the loaves and pies displayed. Most people bought their bread from these shops and Spurriergate was surely a very appetising road, its air permeated with crusty smells. Some confectioners allowed their customers to bring home-made pies for cooking in the bakery oven; a few would only sell their own produce. Delicious confectionery was available from Bayldon and Berry in St Helen's Square. Later Joseph Terry joined the business but fame still lay in the future.

Mr Beckley opened a shop in Thursday market in the autumn of 1813 for the 'grocery and tea trade in all its branches'.

He got enough trade to need several people to work for him; his daunting advertisement demanded: 'Two young men as Assistants in a shop. None need apply who have not been in a respectable situation, and can bring a good character for Honesty, Sobriety, and Industry'. They also had to pay the cost of their application letters; in those stampless days it was normal for the recipient to pay for the letter when collecting it from the Receiving Office but Mr Bleckly's hopefuls were to prepay the postage. They would soon have a young companion for John Bleckly also stated that he had 'room for a clever lad from the Country as an Apprentice'.

The successful candidates would soon be selling cones of sugar wrapped in blue paper, candles from London, hops from Kent and 'Russian Tongues'. They would weigh dried fruit and assure customers that Mr Bleckly had promised that, even if they only bought a pound of currants, they'd be charged at the same rate as those who bought wholesale quantities.

Grocers depended on the arrival of East India Company ships in the port of London with cargoes of tea which were auctioned there; also merchant fleets

Canisters of tea lined the shelves behind the grocer's window

sailing from the West Indies, protected by Royal Navy frigates to save their supplies of sugar, coffee and rum from being stolen by French attackers. It was difficult to estimate when they would arrive. They might crowd all sail in light winds or suffer broken spars in a gale; the crop might be late in ripening or the sugar might dock before previous stores were all sold thus bringing down the price. In February 1815 the price of sugar dropped because there was a rumour that the West India fleet was arriving early. It wasn't, said Mr Bleckly, and exhorted his customers to stock up with his loaf and lump sugar and Fine Strong-grained Jamaica Raws.

His goods certainly came from world-wide. The next year, with the war safely over, he got capers and olives from France as well as rice from Carolina, spermaceti lamp oil from Arctic whales and coffee from the Caribbean.

Not that he neglected home produce. He had cheese from Derby, Cheshire and Wiltshire besides selling Double Gloucester, which he spelt 'Glo'ster'. Some people described themselves simply as cheese-dealers. Not so Mr Bleckly. When the road had been widened from Micklegate to the new Ouse Bridge, he set up a tea warehouse on the corner of Bridge Street.

Of course, there were always people who thought they could buy better or cheaper in London. John Bleckly had no patience with them. He pointed out that the goods had to be insured before travelling to York and, anyway, came from shopkeepers who put up the price to cover their own costly overheads in the capital – or what he called their 'expensive living'. He himself was willing to sell at wholesale prices to anyone who bought at least six pounds of tea. 'Those families,' said Mr Beckly, 'who send to London for their Tea and Groceries pay higher, and are much worse served than they would be in York'.

Anyway, those wanting cheaper food could go to Lucy Sherwood and Mr Monkman who sold rabbits at low prices every day in their Coppergate shop. Or, in 1818, they could go to the sale of Mr Knowlson's stock at cost price – even buying tea canisters and confectionary glasses if they wanted them. If they were afraid of drinking adulterated teas (a real danger) they could patronise Mr Pape opposite the Falcon in Micklegate; he guaranteed that his teas were 'Genuine' as imported; but if one wanted flattering attention, David Sigsworth was the man. He had a shop in Low Ousegate where he trusted he would 'meet with that preference in the Command of Orders, which a generous Public will not fail to shew, according to the merit of his assiduity and attention'.

The young boys of Regency York, in nankeen trousers and buckled shoes, surely gravitated to the corner of Coppergate and Castlegate where the sweet smell of chocolate, mingled with the scent of Turkish coffee, permeated the air. It came from the Tuke grocery shop where it was quite literally a foretaste of what was to come in this city.

The north end of Castlegate, home of the Tukes

But the Tukes were more than grocers; they were tea dealers, too. This meant something prestigious. A tea dealer would go to the capital where the tall-masted ships of the East India Company docked in the Pool of London and their cargoes were auctioned. This was the only official way of obtaining tea in bulk because John Company (the East India Company's nickname) had a monopoly – bringing even the popular China tea in their vessels. No other port was allowed to sell tea and humble grocers couldn't always afford to hire a chaise or travel by stage to London and might not have known what to do when they reached the centre of the world's tea trade. Mr Tuke attended the auctions and bought enough to fill the shelves in his own shop and sell wholesale to grocers in many places.

Tea had already become the national beverage. It was drunk from delicate cups painted with tiny floral sprays and from the popular blue and white ware which imitated Chinese bridges and classical ruins. But it was also the staple drink of poor families who brewed it in the jaundiced glow of tallow candles. Its price was terribly important, eight shillings a pound for 'Flavoured Congoo' and 10 shillings for 'Fine Pekoe Tea', although you could get tea for 4/8d.

Some got it for less. Muffled oars and sunk tea chests led to pistol shots and murdered Preventive Officers on coastal inlets. Those who cheated the Customs might provide cheap tea but they were often deadly shots. Henry Tuke, author of a book on Christian principles, wouldn't touch 'Run' cargoes.

Samuel Tuke was an efficient partner of his father at the shop but Henry died in 1814 and then his son became the chief organiser of the family business. His grandfather, William, lived next-door-but one beside the Robin Hood Inn which, for some reason, has abandoned the leader of the Sherwood Men and is now called after his lieutenant, Little John. Anyway, next door to it lived William Tuke who didn't retire from the grocery business for another four years. Not that he had much spare time for bacon and butter in 1814. . . .

These were the days when the mentally ill were thought 'only fit for Bedlam'. But this kindly grocer had a vision beyond the narrow outlook of the early 19th century. He saw that confinement in spartan surroundings under a harsh régime was the worst possible treatment for a disordered intellect. Even the king had been put in a strait jacket and the Privy Council had given permission for him to be flogged if his mental turbulence was too hard to restrain. But the Christian visionary of Castlegate believed that space and fresh air, compassion and understanding offered the best cure for hurt minds. So he inspired the foundation of The Retreat which became the prototype for good mental hospitals.

He and his family started a Quaker school and also tried to stop the use of Climbing Boys – small lads, covered in soot and sores, who were sent up the inside of chimneys to sweep them.

Nor was that the end of the Tuke family's influence. They gave York something else. You can smell it today if the wind is in the right direction. At the back of Samuel's premises was a workshop where coffee and nuts and chocolate were blended into mouthwatering confectionery and a great-niece of Henry later married Joseph Rowntree II. The Tukes had helped to give York its distinctive flavour.

AN APPEAL

ON

BEHALF OF CLIMBING BOYS.

Printed by William Alexander and Son, Castlegate, York.

Price one ½d.—5d, per dozen—2s. 8d. per hundred.

Ann Alexander's four-page pamphlet about Climbing Boys

VIII

Reading and Remedies

THE GROCER'S DAUGHTER married a bookseller. William Tuke had eight children; Ann was the second child of his second marriage and she became the wife of another William.

He was William Alexander but he wasn't a bookseller when she married him; he was a corn chandler, who took her home to Suffolk but had dreadful difficulties trying to make a living when the war with France upset the corn trade, so he brought Ann back to York and set up business as a bookseller. Ann was back in the street where she was born for William Alexander's shop was number three Castlegate, the opposite side and end from her father.

You can still see the drawing room window if you stand opposite to Stephensons, the estate agents, and look up at the first floor. There, well above the photographs of present day houses for sale, are two charming Georgian windows. The left one belonged to Ann Alexander's drawing room.

Ann Alexander's drawing room window (left)

42

Curved wall forming the back of the curved end of the Alexander's drawing room

When the late afternoon sun shone into that upstairs drawing room, it illuminated the kindly face of William Alexander who was fondling the cat which was sitting on the arm of his high-backed chair. Nearby sat Ann with a tidy little bonnet on her hair. The room still retains that atmosphere of mingled elegance and comfortable domesticity so typical of Georgian England. Its back window gave a view over the cluttered cottage roofs of Water Lane but was set in a bow, cleverly made by putting a curved wall containing a cupboard in each corner. At the opposite end the front window (reaching almost from floor to ceiling) overlooked the busy narrow street and was so near St Mary's Church that the Alexanders surely felt as if they could stretch their hands to touch its stone gargoyles. From time to time the rumbling and clattering of a coach leaving the Robin Hood Inn would shatter the peace of that serene room.

It was shattered by other sounds from the outside world, too; some much more disturbing than the clopping and rattling of the stage. The cry of the little chimney sweeps awoke deep sympathy in the Quaker heart of Ann Alexander. The ragged 'apprentices' were forced up sooty chimneys to clean them by the brutal expedient of lighting a fire in the grate. If they didn't scramble up quickly, they burnt the soles of their feet. It was not unknown for master sweeps to kidnap small boys for the job.

But William and Ann knew there was an alternative to this. John Carey, the joiner in Walmgate, made and sold machines to sweep chimneys. A petition was organised; it consisted of a resolution to use Mr Carey's apparatus in future and it was signed by many shopkeepers and householders, topped by the Mayor and the Dean of York. The Alexanders kept a copy in their shop to persuade their customers to sign it.

They did more. Ann, already an author, wrote a pamphlet setting out the terrible facts about the use of climbing boys and her husband published it in 1817. They had learnt that 'The Pen is mightier than the Sword'. William had added publishing and printing to his bookselling and tried to produce books which would inspire and instruct. The list of his wares includes works on geography, history, theology and printing. People sometimes bought New Year gifts from him for this was a more popular time to give presents than Christmas in Regency days.

He didn't publish novels because he thought them too frivolous and this seems to have caused him to turn down an amazing chance.

Walter Scott had already become a famous and popular author. Local tradition records that the Scottish writer called at the Alexanders' shop whilst he was in York looking at Clifford's Tower and generally doing the research for *Ivanhoe*. Like most authors, he probably automatically gravitated towards bookshops but this one was conveniently near to York Castle and he is said to have struck up a friendship with William, even suggesting that the good Quaker should consider publishing *Ivanhoe*.

William Alexander's staircase

44

'Walter Scott,' said William Alexander, 'I esteem thy friendship, but I fear thy books are too worldly for me to print'.

If the theory is true that the Dr Dryasdust, to whom Scott dedicated *Ivanhoe*, is really Alexander, worldliness wasn't his only objection. He didn't think one could write effectively a novel set in a period so far from living memory. In the preface Scott refuted this criticism but it didn't spoil their friendship and Scott bought in London spectacles required (probably by Ann) in Castlegate.

You didn't get only books from William Alexander. He sold wallpaper, writing desks, umbrellas and 'Miscellaneous Articles', which included portfolios and inkstands.

He wasn't the only bookseller in York. John Wolstenholme had his premises on the corner of Petergate and Minster Gates where his wall has the carving done by his cousin, Francis Wolstenholme of Gillygate. It is a skilful model of Minerva, the Goddess of Wisdom who is appropriately accompanied by that wise-looking bird, the owl. Most bookshops in those days sported Minerva.

If you wanted to read novels, you could get them from John Wolstenholme and lottery tickets as well; but Mr Wolstenholme shared many of William Alexander's humanitarian concerns and the petition to save Climbing Boys could be signed in his shop also. The York Book Society met in his house and planned to start *The Yorkshire Gazette* which he published for the first time in April 1819.

John Wolstenholme's Minerva opposite to John Pickering who sold gloves

In common with York's other booksellers, John Wolstenholme sold much that could be bought from a 'chymist'. He, Spence, Deighton and the Todds, Storry and others had preparations which originated in London and were imported into this city to counteract various maladies. There was Barclay's Ointment for 'that unpleasant and troublesome disorder, the ITCH' and there was advice for the afflicted too. They sold a book for 'The nervous and debilitated of both sexes' which even contained counsel for '. . . those on the eve of Marriage, but whose infirmities are an unsurmountable bar to Connubial Happiness'. Perhaps the 92 year-old bridegroom, whose wedding to a 17 year-old bride was described in the newspaper, bought a copy.

For those seeking marriage Crosby's *Polite Letter Writer or Complete Correspondent* might be a useful book to purchase. It contained 'a great variety of Original Letters, on Friendship, Business, Love and Education'. If you wanted it bound in red, it cost you 2s 6d. Many booksellers sold unbound books so the buyer could order binding to match the colour scheme of his room.

Other enlightening books in stock varied from *An Account of a Voyage to Abysinia (sic)*, the *Speeches of the Rt Hon John Philpot Curran, Master of the Rolls in Ireland* to *The History of the Roman Emperors*. And if those didn't entice the money out of your drawstring purse, there was the *Repository of General Knowledge*, a magazine which taught its readers (among other useful things) Russian etiquette, how to grow Alpine strawberries and details of the scenery in Bombay. Thus edified, the customer could turn his attention to the children for whom *The Royal School Atlas* contained 'problems on maps'. This volume, the publishers claimed, was '. . . the most correct, the most elegant, and at the same time the cheapest, ever executed' and was 'already used in many of the most respectable seminaries in the Empire'.

The Todds, father and sons, had a bookshop in Stonegate sandwiched between Mrs Hopton the corset maker and Mr Palmer the apothecary. You can still see the premises. Find the little red devil on the wall by Coffee Yard; it's attached to the old apothecary's shop and next door to him on the left was John Todd's shop. Even in Regency days it was old – jettied, timbered and latticed.

Nearby lived William Cave whose brother Henry produced a book of beautiful etchings of York. John Todd sold the book which included pictures of his own shop. The shop front was plainer then than now. It has gained more plaster decoration but still proclaims on the upstairs bay window that Bibles have been sold there since 1682.

People could also buy prints – individual pictures which were popular in the days prior to photography. One could purchase prints of nearly everything from African elephants to crude illustrations of the Prince Regent's love life. Gentlemen used to stand looking at the prints stuck on Mr Todd's windows until a chilly wind blowing down Stonegate drove them indoors where a fire in a little black grate at the far end of the room warmed them.

That room had the air of an Oxford college with busts of toga-clad Romans adding extra dignity to the rows of books lining the walls. But Todd's books were not only for the academically advanced. He sold *Guy's School Ciphering Book for Beginners*; it contained 'sums' suitable both for young ladies and young gentlemen and '. . . will save Teachers much needless trouble, both in setting

The bay windows of Todd's first floor with Mrs Hopton's rooms on the left and Palmer's shop on the right

and correcting of such sums,' for, just in case the teacher had his/her problems with 'such sums', an answer book could be bought priced sixpence.

The premises contained at least 30,000 volumes, many of them bound in Morocco leather, and there was the faint but distinctive aroma of leather cured with birch which was imported from Russia for bookbinding. You could find a book to tell you almost anything you wanted to know from the antiquities of Greece to 'the latest improvements and discoveries'. Besides potions and books, one could acquire a picture of the Earl of Dodington's dog kennels 'with striking likenesses of his lordship's Huntsman, Dog-Feeder and some of the most celebrated hounds. . . .'

If you preferred your own likeness to that of his lordship's huntsman, the Todds could show you examples of the work of Mr and Miss Foster who would paint you for three to 10 guineas. And that would be a status symbol because the Fosters claimed to have the patronage of the Duchess of Wellington 'and numerous other distinguished personages. . . .'

Those of a more prosaic disposition went to Todds for rat poison and those whose thirst was not just for knowledge bought lemon acid from them to make into negus, punch or lemonade. It was strongly recommended to owners of taverns and captains of ships.

There was certainly plenty to read in Regency York and plenty of trade for its bookbinders and for the subscription library in St Helen's Square. Horror novels and children's books, herbal medicine and travellers' tales, atlases and Bibles. If it was published, it seemed, York sold it and often printed it as well. The stamping of the press and the clopping of hoofs, the musty smell of books and the crusty smell of bread, the sign of the Bible and the barber's pole – all attracted the senses of York's bonneted and top-hatted shoppers.

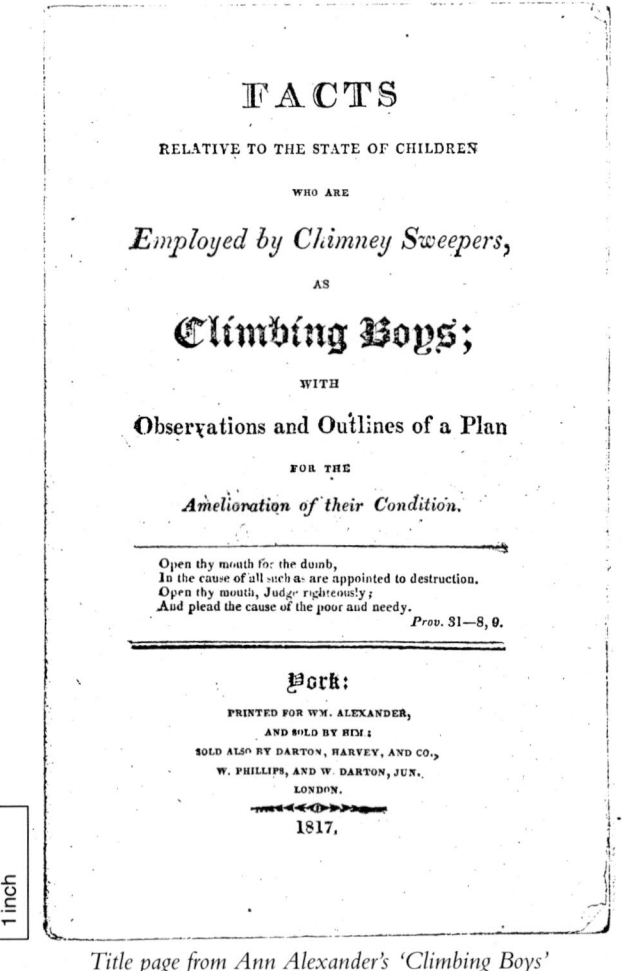

FACTS

RELATIVE TO THE STATE OF CHILDREN

WHO ARE

Employed by Chimney Sweepers,

AS

Climbing Boys;

WITH

Observations and Outlines of a Plan

FOR THE

Amelioration of their Condition.

Open thy mouth for the dumb,
In the cause of all such as are appointed to destruction.
Open thy mouth, Judge righteously;
And plead the cause of the poor and needy.
Prov. 31—8, 9.

York:

PRINTED FOR WM. ALEXANDER,
AND SOLD BY HIM;
SOLD ALSO BY DARTON, HARVEY, AND CO.,
W. PHILLIPS, AND W. DARTON, JUN.
LONDON.

1817.

Title page from Ann Alexander's 'Climbing Boys'

IX

Hats and Hose

A MILLINER'S work was never done; even in the evening hats were worn at assemblies. In fact, a woman's crowning glory was half-hidden most of the time; prospective husbands couldn't see what they were getting – a pig in a poke indeed.

Mr Parsons had a lot to do with the shape of York's hats. In the years before Waterloo he coiffed his ladies with chignons which tucked neatly into their small bonnets. This headgear was horizontal in line with a tiny brim in front and a crown on the back of the head. About the time of Boney's defeat, hairdressers piled their clients' hair high on top and bonnets sported tall crowns and large brims which framed the face becomingly. Inside the brim was lined with ruched silk.

There were also some shapeless hats of twisted taffeta over tortured wire which might drip gloomy black tassels in mourning for a distant and deceased relation, or sport the tail feathers of an unfortunate pheasant shot by dear Papa.

A French fashion print of 1814 depicts a bonnet crowned with huge Madonna lilies and not surprisingly describes it as *merveilleuse et incroyable*.

There can't have been many women who looked beautiful in a Turkish-style turban but there were quite a number who thought they did. And after all one has to be fashionable, my dear, however ridiculous it makes one look. Besides, most young ladies were skilled at altering their milliners' handiwork. Jane Austen, who trimmed bonnets for herself, probably echoed the voices of typical York shoppers when she made Lydia Bennet exclaim, 'Look here, I have bought this bonnet. I do not think it is very pretty; but I thought I might as well buy it as not. I shall pull it to pieces when I get home, and see if I can make it up any better . . . there were two or three much uglier in the shop; and when I have bought some prettier-coloured satin to trim it with fresh, I think it will be very tolerable.'

If she had been at our Mrs Peacock's, she could have bought her satin at the same time. We have already met Mrs Peacock whose daughters travelled to London to fetch samples of the latest in headgear. Since this lady was a dress-maker and haberdasher as well, she is not strictly a milliner but she undoubtedly decorated the heads of many of York's most fashion-conscious ladies.

49

Mrs Peacock and Mrs Morgan were so well-known in York that they often advertised without even giving an address. However, in 1818, when Mrs Peacock's daughter brought the latest bonnets and fabrics from London, there was a notice in the *Herald* 'to acquaint the Ladies of York and its Vicinity' that the delectable goods were 'ready for the inspection of those Ladies who will favour her with a call at her MILLINERY ROOMS, SPURRIERGATE. . . .'

It was not only women who sold bonnets. Mr Cooke spent years in Minster Gates in a welter of ribbons, straw, feathers and flowers. He even sold trimmings and chip hats to country shopkeepers and other milliners. He was half wholesaler and half milliner; not an unusual feature of Regency life and one which he found so profitable that he was able to move into new premises in Coney Street soon after the Regent took the oath.

His new shop was bigger and, although he specialised in straw hats, he was able to offer tippets (little shoulder capes) at prices varying from eight to 14 shillings each. By November he was stocking winter warmth in sable, chinchilla and swansdown. There were bargains to be had, as well, for some of last summer's straw bonnets were reduced to a shilling each; others in finer straw might be 20 shillings. A pound

Bonnet and Spencer shown in a Regency fashion magazine

for a good hat! Yet that was a month's wages for a housemaid who rose at five o'clock each morning to wash floors and black grates.

But Joseph Cooke certainly attracted plenty of customers. Demand was so great that the following year he stocked his shelves with far more, including the very latest fashion – a spencer tippet – which you couldn't get anywhere else in York. A spencer was a tiny little jacket which fitted closely to the bust and didn't even reach the waist; by 1815 the vogue for topping it with a swansdown trimmed tippet was copied by many ladies.

At Cooke's Warehouse you could also get seal skin, ostrich feathers and furry muffs but it still remained the best place to buy straw hats and bonnets priced between seven and 30 shillings. There were black ones and white ones; flowered bonnets and feathered turbans; Dunstable straw and willow hats to say nothing of Italian versions.

If you were hard up, you could get old muffs renovated or buy mock sable at two guineas when the real version was six pounds. Even Black and Silver Bear cost less and Blue Fox might only be a guinea or two pounds. The Hudson's Bay area and Russia provided beautiful furs for a population which hadn't yet learnt to treat animal life and the rest of humankind with the same consideration it gave to its own.

Joseph Cooke didn't do everything himself. His wife began to preside over his showrooms and she had cards printed for distribution to York's ladies advertising tempting millinery confections especially when her husband had returned from Town with the latest collection. In May 1816 he came back replete with chip straw bonnets, poked, high-crowned and beribboned . . . 'Mrs C's show rooms will be fitted up and opened on Monday 27th instant, when the honour of a call will be highly esteemed.'

They were not without competitors; Mr Aspinall's hats and tippets and spencers were good, too, and he had gloves to match.

Some gentlemen's hatters were hosiers as well. Robert Pulleyn, opposite the Mansion House, on the corner of St Helen's Square, sold the best silk stockings, 'gold and silver lace' (which was probably mostly braid), and good quality hats. His position was excellent; gentlemen could get their hair trimmed and anointed with Macassar Oil at Mr Parsons' and then go across to Mr Pulleyn for a fashionable hat to crown it all.

There were plenty of hatters in York, all of them perfectly sane as far as we know! Most of their trade consisted of supplying men with tall felt hats. The most fashionable of these were made of beaver, a hairy-looking felt which you could stroke. The hat was nearly all crown, a forerunner of the Victorian top hat which still goes to Ascot and weddings. The Regency versions were usually brown or black, their brims narrow in comparison with the tall crowns. These varied in shape, some tapered or widened towards the top particularly in the early days of the Regency; the crown grew straighter and taller towards 1820. They were very good for doffing.

At least 13 York hatters supplied them. We can probably get the best idea of one of their shops by studying Lock's in St James's Street, London, where gentlemen's hats have been sold continuously since George III was king. Prospective customers would peer through the little rectangular panes which made up the bowed windows; on shelves besides the glass lay tall beavers with narrow curled brims. The same sort were on view at Hugh Watson's in Coffee Yard, off York's Stonegate, because he got his best headgear from Simpson and Co. and in March 1819 received 'A new supply of Gentlemen's Superfine Hats', so he sold the old beavers at reduced prices. A hopeful purchaser would step into the dim interior and view the hat he fancied in lamplight. It would be taken off its wooden stand and placed reverently on his head. A tall gentleman would need to bend his head when he left through the low doorway (especially if he was already replacing his high hat), although people were on average shorter than we are.

It wasn't only for themselves that gentlemen bought hats; they liked their servants to be dressed in livery which did credit to the status of the employer. Mr Blanchard on the corner of High Ousegate could supply hats in the family livery. Footmen, for instance, wore old-fashioned uniforms topped by a tricorn or bicorn hat lavishly trimmed with gold or silver braid which Regency people would describe as 'frogged with gold lace'.

Mr Blanchard sold so much else besides. In 1819 he purchased cheaply a large stock of partially made hats and then hired a man, trained in London, to finish them.

If your hat was an unfashionable shape, Blanchard could restyle it and if the wind blew it into a puddle, he could clean it, too.

England's damp climate didn't improve beavers but Thomas Pullon sold 'Christy's Superior Waterproof' Gentlemen's Hats. He moved from premises on the corner of Petergate and Stonegate to some newly-built shops in Spurriergate which were patriotically named Waterloo Buildings. Although he sold sealskin forage caps for boys, he specialised in beaver which enabled him to make fashionable riding hats for ladies. A lady would ride side-saddle in a full-skirted habit but her hat resembled her husband's topper with the possible addition of streamers. Whether she bought an elaborate bonnet or a tall riding hat, the customer would carry it away in a bandbox.

When Lydia Bennet bought her ugly bonnet, she and her sisters crammed themselves and their purchases into the carriage and she exclaimed, 'I am glad I bought my bonnet, if it is only for the fun of having another bandbox!'

When our modern shopper hurries along Spurriergate, her plastic bag stamped with the name of a chain store, she follows in the steps of early 19th-century customers who triumphantly carried large drum-shaped bandboxes, Regency-striped, of course.

X

Crispin's Craftsmen

BOOTS boots, boots, boots,
Marching up and down again . . .

That song could just as easily apply to Regency York. Tasselled Hessians tramped the cobbled streets. They got their name from the boots worn by soldiers in the army of the German state of Hesse and they were the most fashionable footwear for men. Youths, who wanted to emulate Beau Brummell, just had to have a pair, though they probably couldn't afford to clean them with a champagne polish as Brummell's valet was reputed to do. They could make do with J. T Rigge's Japan Blacking which, oddly enough, was sold by the pastrycook in Spurriergate but was 'prepared with every ingredient in the most refined state'. Even young men had to sit down sometimes so the Hessians were cut lower at the back allowing the knee to bend. A bootmaker needed to be very skilled.

Then there were the riding boots, hundreds of them. Usually black with a turned-down cuff, they had small tabs to enable a man to pull them on for the well-made ones fitted closely. They were more difficult to clean; a careless polisher got the blacking on the tops but thoughtful waiters and valets didn't clean the brown cuffs until they'd finished burnishing the legs. Then they sponged the brown part with water, reached for the bottle labelled Rank Poison and applied that; this literally vitriolic polish completed the task.

There was probably more demand for the strong laced boots and large shoes worn by workmen. A few professions such as the Law, the Church and the Navy, still used buckled shoes. Shoemakers were needed to make anything from a top boot for riding to hounds to a stout shoe for trudging along muddy lanes but they couldn't all do so.

Probably the aristocratic owners of houses like Micklegate House bought their boots in London from Hoby, for London was said to produce the best. However, if they did wish to purchase some in York, they only had to stroll across the road to Leonard Calvert whose boot and shoe shop was beside the medieval arch on the site of the present Priory Street. We've a clear idea of what it looked like because Henry Cave, the York artist of those days, produced a picture which was printed by his brother William. Unfortunately Henry Cave's picture, which was really drawn to show the old priory gateway, cuts off Mr Calvert's shop half way along its window. Thus it shows a solitary boot, conjuring up a delicious vision of a top-hatted gentleman hopping down Micklegate with an elegant lady on his arm. Perhaps the other half of the pair of boots was farther inside the shop, a foretaste of the modern practice of putting only individual shoes on display when there isn't much space.

Mr Calvert's boot shop beside the Priory gateway

Calvert's son, Thomas, didn't spend his life in the 'gentle craft' for he became a tailor, obtaining his Freedom of the City in 1818 because without that no one could set up in business in York – unless they worked within the Liberty of St Peter where the Minster had jurisdiction. Thomas Calvert would at least know where to send his customers to buy a pair of boots suitable to wear with the trousering he had made for them.

Some Regency Shops specialised in ladies' shoes, others concentrated on male feet whilst a few were general cordwainers as capable of making the saddle as the boots which rested in its stirrups.

A lot might happen behind the scenes; the real shoe 'maker' fixed the sole and heel but the uppers were usually created by the 'clickers' and 'closers'.

York had many curriers, men who cut leather into the shapes required, and some shoemakers bought these cut-outs ready for use. In 1815 Thomas Cochrane, the glover in Blake Street, went bankrupt and his stock was sold cheaply. This included a quantity of leather which was described as 'suitable for shoemakers'. Cochrane was able to continue his business afterwards. Leather became cheaper again in 1817 when its price fell generally and anyway, in a city which had plenty of butchers, there would always be lots of skins for glovers and bootmakers to use.

Fashionable heelless slippers might suddenly be needed in pink or green kid to match the pelisse or gown finished by Steventon and Bownas for a customer who wanted to look just right in Race Week. But it wasn't lucrative to be employed stitching up the silk shoes wanted for balls and assemblies. By 1820 white satin was the favourite for evening wear and ladies bent their heads over fashion drawings which depicted the latest slippers in white satin or corded silk ornamented with clasps of jet or rosettes of pearl.

If you wanted to go to the same shop for both boots and shoes, the Hornbys might be your choice. Richard Hornby worked in Stonegate until January 1815 when he renounced business in favour of his son.

Another Hornby – William – played a prominent part in York life. He'd been one of the people assigned to sort out Thomas Cochrane's assets and was obviously chosen because he was trustworthy and knowledgeable. He signed William Alexander's petition for using a machine instead of a little boy to clean chimneys and was described in the Trade Directory as a gentleman, a name seldom used in those days to describe anyone engaged in trade. A member of the Guild of Cordwainers until it was dissolved, he became a sheriff.

After 31 years making boots and shoes in Blake Street, William Hornby took into partnership three of his foremen – Richard Dale, William Scott and George Dale. Their relationship with him had been a happy one for many years as George Dale could testify, having begun work as an apprentice in Mr Hornby's shop.

However, John Trout, another foreman, left Hornby's in August of the next year and set up on his own account in Coney Street, taking the premises of Mr Sanderson the saddler where, he promised, '. . . the business will be carried on by

Shoemakers at work

him in the neatest manner, and executed with dispatch. Those who please to honor him with their commands, may depend upon the greatest attention being paid to their Orders'.

Not all shoemakers tried to move *into* Coney Street. Mr MacLean left it to find a bigger shop in Castlegate and he certainly chose a location which should bring him trade. His premises were next door to a busy coaching inn; the one we know as the Little John which was the Robin Hood in Mr MacLean's time. Travellers would be sure to notice his windows. Better still, since he sold ladies' shoes, he managed to let lodgings in his house to a Mrs Ridley who made dresses, corsets, pelisses and riding habits 'elegantly ornamented with braid'. Her satisfied customers were bound to want some kid half-boots or similar shoes to match their new outfits. Mr MacLean would have been highly delighted surely when Mrs Ridley answered his advertisement of 'convenient and airy lodgings to let'. She didn't stay with him, however, but moved into a house on Lord Mayor's Walk. Mr MacLean continued to sell shoes in the street of coffee, chocolate and coaches.

In Blake Street you could get shoes from Messrs Bramley and Co whose foreman, William Ellis, left them in 1816 to enter partnership with his wife's husband, Benjamin Clough, the boot and shoemaker in Colliergate. A happy family arrangement perhaps and one which promised advantages for Clough because William Ellis had years of experience with leather and feet.

Mr Clough was in an embarrassing situation during the General Election of 1818. People said he'd accepted money from Sir M. Sykes to help pay for his shop and then voted for the rival candidate. Clough was wild with indignation. It was, he said, 'a false and malicious report' and he hoped his Friends and the Public would exonerate him 'from a charge so vile and ungenerous'.

York had plenty of shoe and bootmakers so there was no need for its citizens to walk slipshod down its medieval streets.

Hessian Boot

XI

Assistants and Apprentices

MR CLOUGH, the shoemaker in Colliergate, was haunted by a fear of combinations. It should, perhaps, be explained that these were the Regency equivalent of trades unions. Mr Clough hated them as much as the British Government did. Terrified that an enthusiasm for decapitating the ruling classes might cross the Channel, Pitt's government had passed the Combination Acts. These didn't actually outlaw combinations, they simply made them toothless by forbidding them to demand higher wages or less hours and making it also illegal to hinder people from working. The conditions applied to employers as well, a diplomatic move unlikely to cause problems for Pitt, Perceval or the Regency premier Lord Liverpool.

Purchases might be delivered for the customer in brown paper parcels

Historical research has shown that the average British working man hadn't the slightest desire to hang any member of 'The Quality' from the nearest lamp bracket; he was horrified by the Revolution. A cartoon of the period typified Mr Average Briton's point of view. It showed the devil's wife giving birth to the French Revolutionaries and satan himself looking shocked. There was no fear of a guillotine being erected in St Helen's Square or anywhere else.

So one may wonder why on earth Mr Clough wouldn't have any members of a combination in his workroom. Well, perhaps he might not have worried if he'd been a hatter or a draper but five groups of workmen ignored the Combination Acts, the shipbuilders, papermakers, printers, tailors, – and shoemakers! During the General Election in Towcester the shoemakers combined with flying fists and rude rhymes against the candidate they didn't like. The London shoemakers had a reputation for demanding higher wages, working when they chose and taking comfort from the bottle. No doubt this was a considerable exaggeration but Benjamin Clough was taking no risks. In his advertisement he said he was '. . . in immediate want of a number of good workmen, who will meet with constant employment on liberal terms. N.B. None need apply who are not entirely free from any combination'.

English craftsmen and shopkeepers (probably unknowingly) used an old French word to describe their employees – journeymen – which meant qualified workmen paid a daily wage, *journée* being the French for day. After finishing their apprenticeship young men usually became journeymen. If there wasn't a vacancy in the shop where they'd been trained, they might advertise for a job like the young draper who inserted this notice in *The York Herald* in March 1812:

TO LINEN-DRAPERS

A young man, who served his apprenticeship, and has been two years journeyman in a well-established shop, and who can be well-recommended by his late master for good abilities, sobriety, and strict attention to business, is in want of a situation, either with a wholesale or retail linen-draper.

Letters, post paid, addressed to the Editors of the York Herald will be immediately attended to.

Sometimes shopkeepers themselves advertised for assistants with a sense of urgency as if plenty of work had suddenly come their way. Mr Rhodes, a tailor in Blake Street was probably facing a rush of work in December 1818, when he said 'Wanted Immediately a Number of Journeymen Tailors' but even so he wouldn't take just anyone. 'None but the best workmen need apply,' he added.

The Tailor's shop

Mr Mallatrat was more specific when he had places for several people: '... those who have been accustomed to any of the principal shops in London, and to the Habit and Pelisse department, will be preferred.'

Frederick Mallatrat had been in partnership with Mr Rhodes, who was his brother-in-law, but they'd parted company when Mr Mallatrat bought a shop in Coney Street (next door to Raper's Bank on the corner of New Street) and then went to London to get the most fashionable stock he could buy.

It was not surprising that he wanted expert journeymen because he intended to make uniforms for naval and military officers. It may be that some of the poppy-coloured coats worn by the Army of Occupation in Paris were made in Coney Street; if so the journeymen needed to be proficient at cutting scarlet cloth (woven in Bradford), applying gold lace, stitching on silver buttons and coloured facings. No wonder that 'none but the best workmen need apply' but Mr Mallatrat did promise them 'the highest wages'. He inserted the advertisement in the newspapers several weeks in succession so perhaps he wasn't overwhelmed with suitable applicants.

But he scored a great triumph. He obtained as a foreman someone who had worked for years in London's top tailoring establishments including the firm of Weston who achieved fame making Beau Brummell's superbly fitting coats.

An opportunity occurred when he wanted an apprentice for the training promised would be stylish and the lad would be allowed to work there until he was eligible to apply to be a Freeman of the City of York and set up his own business. Moreover, Mr Mallatrat promised to treat him 'as one of the Family'. We don't know how attractive that proposition was. The tailor took his work seriously and didn't even use his own vaulted wine cellar but let it to someone else. He insisted that the hopeful apprentice should have 'respectable connections'.

That was not an unusual stipulation.

Apprenticeship could be anything from cheap labour for a canny master to a superb technical training for a youth destined to be a York version of Dick Whittington. After several years ominously called 'servitude' the apprentice would become a fully qualified journeyman. At that stage he was eligible to be 'made free'; this didn't mean that the slave got his liberty – it indicated that the trained assistant became a Freeman of the city and ultimately some Freemen were elected to the office of Lord Mayor.

The opposite extreme faced the pauper apprentice who passed from the local parish authority to a shopkeeper who probably gave more orders and cuffs than

The apprentice might act as a delivery boy among other chores

training and board. Some apprentices simply 'legged it' and the masters didn't let them go easily.

A Boroughbridge baker put a notice into *The York Herald* when George Green, his apprentice, ran off. 'He had on when he left, a drab coat, red waistcoat, and corduroy breeches, is about 5 feet 3 inches high, 18 years of age, stiff made with brown hair and ruddy complexion. Whoever will give information of the above apprentice, to Edward Gatenby, of Boroughbridge, shall be well rewarded; and,' added Mr Gatenby who believed in using both the carrot and the stick, 'any person harbouring him after this notice will be Prosecuted.' George probably had another three years servitude due because apprentices were usually 'bound' until they were 21.

Mr Linfoot, a Strensall carpenter, left no one in doubt about his feelings when his apprentice escaped. People were adjured to hunt for a tall swarthy lad and take immediate action when they found him. 'Whoever will apprehend the said apprentice, and Lodge him in any of his Majesty's gaols, shall be well rewarded by applying to the said Ralph Linfoot; and any person harbouring or employing him after this notice, shall be prosecuted according to Law.'

Local government centred on the parish which had responsibility for orphaned and destitute children living there. Since the feeding and clothing of them was an expense, it was cheaper to apprentice them to a trade. If the future master lived out of the locality, he could receive £5 for taking the child; if he was a local he didn't have to be paid. The Overseers of the Poor were the officials responsible for making the arrangements.

A few days before Waterloo the Overseers of the Parish of All Saints, Pavement announced that they had six boys whom they wished to place out as apprentices.

The poor apprentice was regarded as his master's property. If he was captured by the Press Gang and found himself on board a 'Heart of Oak' battling with the French, his Navy wage (such as it was) could be paid to his master. Property meant more than human welfare in Georgian England.

Sometimes a father was willing to pay a shopkeeper to take his lad as an apprentice. In this case, the boy's interests might be considered. A skilful shopkeeper, who could teach a lad his trade, might set him up for life, might even take him into partnership eventually. Ideally the apprentice was treated like an adopted son but his father had to pay the master a fee. Hopeful parents studied advertisements until a suitable situation was found.

Varied apprenticeships were offered in York. Ferrand and Dodgson, the carvers and gilders in Spurriergate, wanted an apprentice in their workroom where 'busts and figurines' were made to ornament the mantlepieces of St Saviourgate and Bootham. Prests, the apothecaries, wanted 'a well-educated Youth, as an apprentice to a surgeon and apothecary in extensive practice'. The sister-in-law of Henry Cave, who left us such useful drawings of Regency York, wanted an apprentice when she was widowed because she and her son meant to continue William Cave's business as an engraver.

In 1817, Mr Sweeting the draper wanted an apprentice and said, 'A stout youth, about 15 years of age, would be preferred'. He wasn't advertising for a Billy Bunter; Regency people used the word stout to indicate health and strength. If you were 'feeling stout' you were quite well.

A Regency shop interior

XII

Medicine Men

York's 'chymists' sold Oxley's Concentrated Essence of Jamaica Ginger which was 'in constant use with many persons of the Highest rank and respectability', doubtless because 'It relieves and shortens the duration of fits of the gout, confining them to the extremities and mitigating the paroxysms' and thereby obviating the need to order the carriage to take one to Harrogate to drink the waters of 'The Stinking Spaw'.

The chemists were joined, as we have seen, by the booksellers in selling various remedies. Among them was that great Regency cure-all Daffy's Elixir, not to mention Dr Anderson's Scotts Pills (30 in a box), Squire's Grand Elixir, Golden and Plain Spirits of Scurvy-grass, Bateman's Drops and Dr Lockyet's Pills.

For 'deranged action of the stomach' due to colds or excessive eating and drinking resulting in 'sickness, jaundice, windy disorders, indigestion, etc' Anti-bilious Pills were on sale. Some people relied on rhubarb tablets and these could be obtained in tiny round boxes. One of their most illustrious users was the Duke of Wellington and there is at Apsley House, his London home, a box containing one or two which he never required. York people might prefer to rely on a local preparation made by the Knaresborough chemist, Mr Ellis, for they were encouragingly informed that 'scarcely any complaint of the stomach and bowels can resist it'.

If your trouble was more of a bronchial nature, you might ask for the Regency version of linctus. The advertisement explained that 'The principle organs not only inhale the matter of life and animation under the form of Oxygen, but at the same time expel from the system the vitiated principle, the foe to health and even existence. How essential then to the human frame is a healthy state of the Lungs, and what gratitude is due to the hand that offers a certain remedy for pectoral diseases'. The hypochondriac, concerned about expelling his vitiated principle, could express his gratitude to a certain Mr Ramsay by buying his Pectoral Balsam.

A typical 'chymist' of the period had rows of small wooden drawers behind his counter, each painted with the name of its contents arranged alphabetically.

The shop of Mr Palmer the apothecary

One of York's foremost restorers of health was the apothecary, Mr Palmer, who worked next door to Todd's bookshop. You can see his shop today if you pause by the entrance to Coffee Yard where the red devil (sign of the printers who once populated the area) is fixed to the apothecary's wall; his premises now house a tasteful gift shop. When Henry Cave drew the building in 1813, he had to copy many little details which have disappeared now; the outside of Mr Palmer's shop was elaborately decorated with carved wood and moulded plaster. It certainly didn't appear clinical although one of his contemporaries said it was: 'Bespread with a barbarous mixture of Grecian architectural ornament and others neither Gothic nor Grecian; while an embroidery of foliage and scroll-work appears to be crammed on every part susceptible of ornament. . . .' Far more important to the Regency public was the bay window with its jars and bottles.

The faint-hearted might not like everything on Mr Palmer's premises. He would certainly possess more than one leech; the fat wormlike creature lived in a jar with a perforated lid to let it breathe.

Inside the low ceiling was crossed by oak beams, part of the timber structure, for Mr Palmer's premises were very old even in Regency times. He would certainly use several pestle and mortars whilst small weighing scales would be needed for assessing the correct quantities in his medicines.

Then, as now, England's weather provoked aches and pains. These were exacerbated by poverty in an age when there were no state benefits. During the severe snow of February 1814 the poor were advised that 'there is a simple method of continuing heat long after the fire has gone out. If a brick is placed for some hours on the hob of a grate, or close to a fire, so as not to lie too hot to be handled, and is wrapped up for the sake of cleanliness in a sheet of whitey-brown paper, and then put in a couple of yards of coarse flannel; when placed between the sheets of a bed near the feet, it will communicate its warmth for 7 or 8 hours, and will in some degree make up for a proper covering'. It is no wonder that the poor often suffered from consumption, as TB was then called. At least they were allowed to buy Vegetable Balsam at cost price since that was considered the best cure.

However, rich living created its own problems but Sutcliffe and Company had the answers. 'Their Ginger Beer is one of the finest Stomachics.' And, if that wasn't good enough, they could help you to copy Lord Byron's diet of soda water and biscuits. It didn't save him from the innuendoes of society but he reckoned it did wonders for his system after too much imbibing. Sutcliffes sold patent Soda Water in glass bottles. If matters became desperate there was always castor oil – though it might be wiser to buy Dr Taylor's Restorative PIlls recommended for a variety of maladies and claimed to be 'a counterpoise against that grand enemy of man, INTEMPERANCE'. Sutcliffes assured the public that everything they sold was of the first Quality. This didn't only refer to drugs. In May 1814 their

Spruce Beer was said to be 'in the highest perfection' and, if you'd had recourse to the dreaded castor oil, they could refresh you with lemonade.

A foretaste of today, the citizens of Regency York could get Schweppes mineral waters which cost 9 shillings and 6 pence a dozen. Harton and Co. had what we should call the franchise; you couldn't get your Schweppes anywhere else in York.

The renumeration of an apothecary was certainly not princely. In 1817 William Forbes was in very low spirits trying to support a wife and seven children. Eventually it all became too much for him and his patients were told that 'it became absolutely necessary to send him to a Proper Place to be taken care of'. The banks and the library collected donations for his family because, the newspaper said that their 'only source of support was the income derived from his Profession, which was scarcely adequate to their maintenance'. York people were generous and Frances, his wife, used their subscriptions to set up a grocery business.

Some customers, arriving at the chemist's shop, knew exactly what they wanted because they'd read *Solomon's Guide to Health*. There they got alphabetical advice on everything from Appetite, loss of, through Green Sickness, Flatulence or Wind, Hypochondria or Melancholy Complaints, to Rheumatism and Turn of Life. This helped them to know whether to get Whitehead's Celebrated Essence of Mustard from Mr Spence or Swainson's Vegetable Syrup of De Velnos from Mr Wolstenholme. If in doubt, the latter was probably the best since its inventor assured the prospective purchasers that 'since the Days of the Deluge no Remedy has been discovered so truly efficacious . . . in the cure . . . of any of the melancholy diseases which originate in impurity of the blood and juices'.

Chemists, then as now, sold beauty aids. Hubert's Roseate Powder got rid of hairs on the face. Described as 'an elegant Article', this depilatory was sold by several of York's druggists. One of them was Champlay who also stocked Ching's Patent Worm Lozenges. In fact, he seems to have had a particular concern about this malady for he also sold 'Ramsay's Medicated Spice Nuts for Destroying Worms' which had the added advantage of tasting good so children were willing to be dosed with them.

Mr Champlay's shop was in Low Ousegate which was widened when Ouse Bridge was rebuilt. In 1819 he was at 17 New Bridge Street where he was succeeded by a Mr Hardman.

Miss Dancer sold Macassar Oil which was claimed to give long lustrous curls and was said to be so 'innocent' that it might be used on the smallest child; but one can't help feeling that ladies needed to be cautious about applying something which 'Promotes the growth of Whiskers, Eyebrows and Mustachos'.

Miss Dancer's Coney Street shop was officially a perfumier's but she stocked Staughton's Elixir, Friar's Balsam, Pike's ointment and Beaume de Vie besides preparations designed to help the worm-eaten, the bald and the rat-infested. A useful lady.

An apothecary's shop was a kind of health centre where diagnosis and advice were given, although some of the remedies offered were probably more dangerous than the diseases they were meant to cure. The typical apothecary sold patent

Henry Cave's drawing of Mr Palmer's Shop with jars of remedies in the window

medicines for which the most astounding claims were made by their inventors. No one had heard of a virus, sheep's dung was considered a useful remedy whilst various roots were crushed, powdered and weighed to produce potions taken by great-grandpapa who probably had no relief from his trouble.

Nevertheless, it was in George III's reign that modern medicine really began. It was begun by two surgeons, the Hunter brothers, who taught their students to keep meticulous records of the effects of treatment upon their patients. The stethoscope was invented in France in 1819 but the best that could be used in Regency York would be a watch with a minute hand which allowed Mr Prest, Mr Palmer and others to take the patient's pulse.

The hopeful customer would survey shelves of jars and drawers labelled 'opium' and 'aloes'. In the background the apprentice might be grinding with pestle and mortar or keeping accounts with a quill pen. He was learning from his employer's experience and the accumulated wisdom of the generations which could produce many benefits like digitalis, the effective heart remedy culled from foxgloves. Mr Cautley, the druggist in Low Ousegate, wanted an apprentice in 1813, and again three years later, and another in 1820.

Throughout the Regency, Keats was apprenticed to a London surgeon and some of his earliest poetry was composed then but most apprentices were not occupied with imperishable verse; they were learning the 'trade'.

In 1815, by the Apothecaries Act, Parliament gave the Society of Apothecaries powers to insist that apprentices attended some lectures, worked for a while in a hospital and sat a written examination. It was rudimentary by our standards but it changed a shop assistant into a doctor.

Not all chemists had the same preparation for the job. Mr Raimes served as doctor on board a whaler in the Arctic cold – probably not bad training for one who was to dispense ointment for chilblains, cuts and sprains.

Your chemist could support you in more than one way. Trusses were the merchandise of James Baker who sold 'the new invented serpentine curved and other spring trusses'. One of his specialities was called significantly the Naval Truss. It was probably in great demand when seamen raced up the ratlines and along the spars to furl flapping canvas in a Force Nine gale and the look-out was posted to the crow's nest scanning the horizon for a strange sail. There were more men injured by dropping from the rigging and falling on the decks than ever were wounded by the French.

Plenty of 'chymists' certainly weren't doctors but sold well-tried 'receipts'. Most of their preparations came in bottles from London and elsewhere. Church's Cough Drops was a ubiquitous remedy (the guard on the Birmingham to Sheffield mail coach said they saved his life) but Spurr and Lockwood were the only people in York to sell Hellmenthe Chorion Syrup which was popular in France, Spain, Italy and Germany. What for? Worms again.

XIII

Chairs and Chattels

REGENCY CABINET-MAKERS might be described as Most Elegant Copy-cats. In the 18th century it had been fashionable to use Chinese and ancient Roman motifs to decorate English furniture; by the Regency complete imitations of classical Roman and Greek furniture were very popular. Although the British had to wait another 150 years for package holidays, the wealthy Englishman abroad was already a feature of continental life. He often managed to buy, or otherwise acquire, real and fake antiquities. These became the inspiration of furniture designers whose pattern books were even used by provincial craftsmen.

Similarly, although it would be another hundred years before Howard Carter found wonderful things in the Valley of the Kings, Napoleon had attacked Egypt where the French discovered the Rosetta Stone. Subsequently Nelson defeated the French fleet in a brilliant action at Aboukir Bay. Regency styles reflected these doings and sphinxes began to support the arms of British chairs. Gilded bronze was used to add scarabs and figures wearing Egyptian head-dresses to sideboards, tables and chairs.

Medieval styles were copied as well. They were known as Gothic and delighted readers of the fashionable novels about knights and jousting, monks and abbeys. The popularity of such books as *Ivanhoe* led to a demand for chairs with backs like Early English arches. When Thomas and George Beal at the furniture shop in Stonegate advertised 'a curious old cabinet', they would certainly attract customers. Mr Dodgson in Coney Street sold old pictures to add more atmosphere.

Looking-glasses which matched the room (Greek, Roman, Egyptian, Chinese or Medieval) were in demand. David Doeg in St Saviourgate was one of York's chief mirror-makers and James Cloak, his apprentice, obtained the Freedom of the City in 1812. Then there was Joseph Brocklebank who shared Mr Doeg's premises and was able to get consignments of excellent wood from him whilst David Doeg was in London.

Mahogany and satinwood were in constant use but more exotic woods were imported, too. Amboyna, calamander, ebony, kingwood, rosewood and zebrawood reflected Britain's trade with Brazil, Ceylon, India and the Indies (both East and West). But mahogany remained the most popular choice.

A Cabinet-maker

In narrow little Peter Lane (nearly opposite the modern shop, Dixons) John Middleton had his lamplit premises. There you could buy elegant mahogany chairs and strong chests of drawers. He also sold clothes presses which were large cupboards doing the duty of a modern wardrobe; clothes were laid flat on their shelves instead of hanging as they do now. Mr Middleton also supplied everything to give you a good night – the bedstead, its feather mattress, bolster and pillows, plus blankets and chintz hangings. Even the fender, fire-irons and tea-tray could be purchased from the same shop since cabinet-makers didn't define furniture so narrowly as we do; they sold most things wanted in a room.

Not that John Middleton made a great profit. In 1812 he was bankrupt and his stock was sold each day from 10 o'clock onwards throughout the week beginning March 23rd. Other cabinet-makers were advised to inspect the wood for sale as there was plenty of mahogany and seasoned planks. Some furniture was made with a beautiful mahogany front but plankwood at the back where it stood against the wall.

York's furniture shops would be sweetened by the honeyed smell of beeswax rubbed into bedposts, window-seats and dainty bureaux. The surfaces of the many types of table gleamed with it. These included all those with folding flaps, such as games tables and sofa tables, plus the various circular ones which usually ended in a monopodium decorated with Greek acanthus or supported on Roman lions' heads.

Naturally the English posterior could not find comfort on a hard Roman-style seat so designers used their ingenuity to produce an upholstered classical chair. A purist wouldn't have had one in the house but many Regency ladies were glad to sit on something which looked as if it could have been unearthed from Pompeii but had the comfort of a padded seat covered in Lancashire cotton damask. The lady in our picture is the epitome of Regency taste – that odd mixture of Graeco-Roman with essential English. The simple lines of her gown imitate the Grecian maiden whilst her bonnet is trimmed with modern lace and cottage flowers. This illustration was printed in *Ackermann's Repository of the Arts* (1819) which was the high-class journal of those days. It helped to promote the classical mode, even giving its models Roman noses!

Imitating the Greeks became even more fashionable than copying the Romans. In his 'Ode to a Grecian Urn', Keats described an ancient vase decorated with figures which would appeal to the Regency taste.

A lady on a Roman-style chair

'Oh Attick shape! Fair attitude! with brede
Of marble men and maidens overwrought . . .'

Studying such antique pottery gave furniture designers ideas to copy and Regency ladies something to want. Longing for a perfectly classical chair which she couldn't afford probably produced a different type of overwrought maiden in York, one who had recourse to Dr Brodrum's Nervous Cordial. If she did purchase a chair with a lyre-shaped back, she couldn't produce an exact musical accompaniment but she probably played the harp and went to Mr Knapton in Coney Street who sold 'an EXCELLENT ASSORTMENT OF HARP STRINGS' according to his advertisement.

Even a barometer might be shaped like a lyre but you needn't enter a shop to buy one. Children were familiar with the rhyme of the street vendor who passed the timbered houses with a clock under his arm and a barometer in his hand, calling:

'Who buys a clock to keep the time,
   Or weather-glass so neat,
 They both are good, and each will chime
   So true without deceit.'

Not perhaps worthy of Keats but practical.

Most of the pseudo-classical chairs had outward-turning legs. The backs were usually straight at the top but sofas had scroll-shaped ends. These were usually covered in velvet or silk which was often embroidered. An expensive version was buttercup yellow stitched with silver leaves and small pink flowers. In less affluent homes cottons would substitute for silk; they could be very pretty and even a duchess chose a rose-patterned chintz instead of satin. But it was generally conceded that libraries and dining-rooms needed a serviceable cloth, scarlet and crimson were popular.

York customers could get their upholstery from King's; when old Mr King died, his son took over the business in Swinegate whilst Jane King opened a shop in Goodramgate.

John Bellerby, in Micklegate, boasted the support of the 'Nobility, Gentry and the Whole of his Friends'; he was probably in a good position to attract this elevated custom since some county families had town houses in that road.

Also in Micklegate were Messrs Ellis and Rusby who not only upholstered your seat but made your coffin, too – that is until they parted company and Hugh Rusby bought Francis Ellis out.

Mrs Marshall, in Coney Street, supplied wooden furniture with beautifully turned legs. She also sold gentlemen's dressing cases, ladies' work boxes and even fans and jewellery.

Some craftsmen specialised in turning legs for chairs

Perhaps John Taylor in Peter Lane surpassed them all for variety. An undertaker in every sense of the word, he sold nearly anything you could lay your hands on, literally, including 'a good pianoforte' and 'IMPROVED UPRIGHT MANGLES, which, for portability and ease, excel any hitherto offered for the public'.

Cabinet-makers needed extensive premises like those belonging to William Sollitt in Jubbergate which comprised his own home, a shop for his customers to enter, a yard for horse-drawn carts to fetch and carry his wares, a shed to store his timber and workshop where the furniture could be made. These are the sort of premises which once stood where the open space of Parliament Street is today.

Besides furnishing rooms, York shopkeepers catered for their floors and windows. Wall to wall carpets are a modern luxury. Regency rooms had a square carpet with a wooden surround which harboured dust and needed frequent mopping but the carpets were often beautiful. Many were made in this county, also in Scotland and in Kidderminster. All these, with expensive examples from Brussels, were available from John Mush near Monk Bar. He would send patterns for his customers to select their choice and he could provide wallpaper to tone with the carpet. He stocked 'paper hangings' designed by French artists and acquired others from London, besides making his own.

The material for curtains would be purchased at the drapers' but the fashionable housewife then wanted fringes and tassels to tie the drapes. Dean

A pianoforte would be highly valued

Wolstenholme made fringes and Francis Wolstenholme carved, moulded and gilded to decorate walls with elegant touches. His premises are still there in Gillygate near to the junction with Bootham. Standing with your back to the traffic lights and looking upwards and leftwards, you can see his halfmoon-shaped windows above slight bows, like a pair of Georgian eyes surveying the modern shoppers.

Francis Wolstenholme's premises in Gillygate still show some of his plasterwork above the windows

XIV

Gleam of Gold

THE LADY'S WHITE SATIN GOWN wafted and hushed in time to the movements of the decorous minuet; it whirled and glinted when she raised her arm to catch her partner's hand in the breathless country dance. Throughout the evening in the Assembly Rooms the shimmering dress remained artistically decorated with a fashionable pale green stole called a 'drapery of crape' which lifted and fell as the young woman gyrated or side-stepped in the movements of reel and cotillion. But the elegant green drapery didn't slip off; it was secured on the shoulder by an amber brooch . . .

. . . purchased very probably from Edward Jackson, one of York's most eminent jewellers. If he hadn't an amber brooch, cornelian would be as good; both stones were fashionable along with amethyst, topaz and turquoise, coral and jet. There were many middle-class ladies who wished to wear stylish jewellery but couldn't afford the emeralds and rubies which passed as heirlooms down noble families. New fashions were developed by the Regency jewellers enabling the vicar's daughter and the cabinet-maker's wife to choose a yellow topaz cross or a brooch of pink garnets.

Pearls were particularly popular. They lustred the throat and shone from the ears; they even

Gowned for the evening and wearing a pearl necklace, 1817

76

formed buttons and rosettes on evening gowns. Mr Jackson bought and sold pearls at his shop in Coney Street appropriately near the bank which was situated on the corner of New Street. There, too, he sold diamonds and coloured gems. In his shop one could spend or recoup a small fortune. Strange coins were in circulation, some of them not legal currency. If you were unlucky, you might have a pocketful of useless silver but Mr Jackson could help you. The inspectors might not accept them as legal tender but he was willing to give good money for dubious foreign coins brought to him because he could melt the silver and use it; he was a gold and silversmith as well as a jeweller. If your great-grandmother left you a hideous diamond parure, he would buy that from you, too. Not that anyone was likely to be so festooned in diamonds as Queen Charlotte when her lilac gown almost disappeared from sight under the weight of a diamond stomacher, necklace, earrings, head-dress, and five bands of diamonds terminating in tassels, 'all the diamond and pearl bands and chains being displayed to great advantage by being placed on wreaths of purple jessamine leaves,' said the *Lady's Magazine*. Fortunately her humbler subjects in York were usually content with coral beads.

Mr Jackson did, however, solicit the patronage of the local aristocracy. He had been head of the workforce at Cattle and Barber's (of whom more anon) and had experience in London which was always a magic formula for getting custom in York. He even had workmen who had been trained in the metropolis so he claimed to be capable of making anything which anybody wanted.

And that certainly would include the use of jet – very likely from Whitby. It was not only the broken-hearted who went into black for a family death. The most distant and unloved relation cast all the females into black bombazine and jet beads. Mr Jackson gloomily announced 'A fashionable assortment of Mourning Rings . . . always kept ready for inspection'.

On a more cheerful note, he promised to restring your pearls or reset your coloured gems. He was also willing to take 'an active steady youth' as an apprentice.

More than any of these things, the modish lady wanted at least one cameo. Nothing could make her look so like a Roman or Greek maiden as a cameo. Clever jewellers cut delicate shells to form small portraits for brooches, rings and even tiaras. Some of them were carved into charming reproductions of pretty women's faces; far more were chiselled into formidable profiles of Roman matrons (all long-nosed) and Greek goddesses (with metallic-looking helmets). These cameos might be set in chunky gold and silver or in delicate filigree.

York had several silversmiths; some of them, like Mr Astley, were also jewellers and goldsmiths. Astley seems to have moved around. In October 1813 he went next-door-but-one in Spurriergate where he promised that no exertions would be wanting to satisfy his Friends and the Public. By 1818 his friends and the public could find him in Jubbergate, at least that was his address when he voted in the General Election. Perhaps there wasn't enough trade in Spurriergate for him and William Anley, another silversmith there, who also had a reputation as a watchmaker.

Jewellery and watchmaking didn't always run in families. Isaiah Creasor, the silversmith, was an innkeeper's son and Thomas Cressey, the watchmaker, was a farmer's boy.

George Hoy was another who moved; he'd had premises on Ouse Bridge and when that was widened and modernised people like Mr Hoy had to quit. He settled in Micklegate in October 1817 and there you could take your watch to be repaired; he even attended to church clocks. Eighteen months later he died but his wife, Elizabeth, carried on his business. There were many women shopkeepers in Regency days, mostly widows who had inherited a thriving concern and managed to keep it going, often with the help of sons, partners or apprentices.

If you wanted a musical clock, Mr Watson was your man. In 1819 he took the shop which had been a hatter's in Stonegate so, although one could no longer get a curly-brimmed beaver there, one could buy a fob-watch. All watches hung from chains or lived in pockets; no one had yet thought of a wrist watch.

Robert Cattle and James Barber in Coney Street were in partnership as jewellers, watchmakers, silversmiths and goldsmiths. A prosperous firm, they were very respected and occupied an important place in York's commercial life. Mr Cattle was chosen as executor of the estate of the printer, Bartholoman. Cattle and Barber also performed a very useful function in those days of, literally, small change. Throughout Georgian times we never had enough coinage. It became very difficult to pay for anything cheap. You just didn't have the cash in your purse. And that didn't mean you were poor; there could be a wad of banknotes in your pocketbook and your creditworthiness might be beyond doubt – you still hadn't any pennies or shillings. The country was so short of specie at one time that we used Spanish coins and stamped over them the English denomination they represented. Some employers hadn't the right coinage to pay their workmen each week so they had to give fortnightly wages instead.

This is where a firm like Cattle and Barber could be so useful. A wealthy businessman with enough gold for security could issue tokens which he was willing to redeem for the amount stamped on them. The fact that he was able to redeem them at face value meant that his customers were prepared to accept his tokens and use them in payment themselves. Anyone accepting them knew that they could cash them at the issuer's premises and so they circulated as currency in the neighbourhood. Cattle and Barber were the only people to issue silver tokens in York, although some other firms made copper tokens.

In 1811 Cattle and Barber issued silver shilling and sixpenny tokens. These had the value and the firm's name on one side and York's coat-of-arms on the other. Unfortunately some forgers made copper fakes, coated with silver, which circulated in the city but people were warned to feel the weight of their tokens since the copper weighed heavier than the genuine light silver ones.

A Cattle and Barber silver token shilling, 1811

The jewellers wanted an extra hand in the watch department and advertised for someone with experience and 'an unexceptionable character'. This paragon would be rewarded with 'liberal encouragement' which presumably meant good wages. A few months later he might be working for Mr Cattle *or* Mr Barber, but not both.

Their partnership was dissolved on the first day of 1814. James Barber undertook to pay any money they owed and receive any debts owing to them. One of their trusted assistants, William Whitwell, became Mr Barber's new partner.

The split caused problems about the tokens as they had been issued in the name of a partnership which no longer existed. So Mr Barber took legal advice. The upshot was that people who held shillings and sixpences in the name of Cattle and Barber were told to take them to the Savings Bank on the 14th and 15th March (1817) and they would receive their nominal value. After that date the old issue would be worthless.

Barber and Whitwell's neighbour was Mr Pullon, the aptly named hatter, two years later Edward Westoby was exhibiting his miniature paintings at their premises. Some of the silverware made by Barber and Whitwell still exists including an apple-corer, very useful for the Regency cook whose recipe began, 'Prepare twenty golden pippins . . .'

The various silversmiths could have their workmanship tested and marked with York's assay mark which included both the city arms and a crowned leopard – a sign of approval for jewellers from a gem of a city.

XV

Who Was Where?

THE NOSE OF A BLOODHOUND would be needed to sniff out the exact whereabouts of many of our Regency shopkeepers. The modern snooper is hampered because so few buildings were numbered. Advertisements don't help as much as one hopes because York had a relatively small population so people mostly knew where a particular shop was. They didn't need to be told and, if they did, a simple comment sufficed, such as, 'Next door to Mr So-and-so'.

Some warehouse owners rented their property from the Dean and Chapter and their leases still exist but even here there is a certain vagueness because the streets themselves have altered. William Tuke's property (which he built himself) is described as a 'Messuage House or Tenement situate in Coppergate Nooke and opening thereunto and into Castlegate . . .' The charmingly sounding Coppergate Nooke would be hard to find today. For his house with all its 'Cellars Sollars Lofts Backsides Commodities Easements and Appurtenances' William Tuke had to pay 'eight shillings of lawful money of Great Britain upon Haxby's Tomb' in the Minster 'at the Feasts of Pentecost and St Martin the Bishop in Winter by even and equal proportions'. Most Georgian writers seemed to make up in capital letters what they omitted in commas!

When Mr Kingan started selling groceries and fruit in Thursday Market, all he needed to say was that he 'has taken the shop lately occupied by Mr John Johnson'. To those of us never privileged to have met Mr Johnson it is hard to know precisely where Mr Kingan was; yet we are sure that when we cross St Sampson's Square to reach Brown's we are very near his old shop – possibly on the very spot where he sought the 'patronage and support' of 'his Friends and the Public'. No doubt the errand boy, for whom he advertised, was never told to go to Number 3 Castlegate. It would be a case of 'Take this to Mr Alexander and look sharp about it because, when you come back from there, you're to go to Mr Potts'. It would be a bold errand boy who dared to ask where Mr Potts lived. And he wouldn't need to do so because Mr Potts was the watchmaker next door to the White Swan, Goodramgate.

Everybody knew that!

Just as the lady shopping in Coney Street knew exactly where the Misses Bickers and Sowerby had their new selection of dress materials recently delivered from the capital; since they said that they would be obliged by 'the honour of a call', she hurried along to give them that honour. Then there would be time to visit a milliner before returning home to Micklegate. Something smart would be required to wear with one's purple shawl – something large and black and feathered. Mrs Peacock would have the very thing. No wonder she called her Millinery rooms by the name of London House! And how fortunate that she was situated so near the pastrycook for, after buying the bonnet, there would be time to call at Mr Elliott's to order one of his Game and Goose Pies.

Off to Spurriergate!

Something large and black and feathered from Mrs Peacock and then off to Mr Ellis for a pie to take home

Bibliography

ACKWORTH, *Margaretta Ackworth's Cookery Book*, edited A. and F. Prochaska (Pavilion Books/Michael Joseph, 1987)
ADAMS, Samuel and Sarah, *The Complete Servant*, edited Pamela Horn (Southern Press, 1989)
ALDBURGHAM, Alison, *Shops and Shopping* (1981)
AIKEN HODGE, Jane, *The Private World of Georgette Heyer* (The Bodley Head, 1984)
ALLOTT, Stephen, *Friends in York* (Sessions of York, 1978)
ARLOTT, John, *The Snuff Shop* (Michael Joseph, 1974)
ASHTON, John, *The Dawn of the Nineteenth Century in England* (T. Fisher Unwin, 1906)
AUSTEN, Jane, *Emma* (1816)
AUSTEN, Jane, *Northanger Abbey* (1818)
AUSTEN, Jane, *Pride and Prejudice* (1813)
BEBB, Prudence, *Life in Regency York* (Sessions of York, 1992)
BURKE, Thomas, *The Streets of London* (Batsford, 1940)
BUTTERY, Darrell, *The Vanished Buildings of York*
BURTON, Elizabeth, *The Georgians at Home* (Longmans, 1967)
CHANDLER, George, *Four Centuries of Banking* (Batsford, 1968)
COLLARD, Frances, *Regency Furniture* (Antique Collectors Club, 1985)
CRUIKSHANK, Dan, *A Guide to the Georgian Buildings of England and Ireland* (Weidenfeld and Nicholson, 1985)
CRUIKSHANK, Dan, and BURTON, Neil, *Life in the Georgian City* (Viking, 1990)
CUNNINGTON, Willett and Phillis, *The History of Underclothes* (Michael Joseph, 1951)
DAVIS, Dorothy, *History of Shopping* (1966)
DURBIN, Gail, *Wigs, Hairdressing and Shaving Bygones* (Shire Publications, 1984)
EDWARDS, Ralph, and RAMSEY, L. G. G., *The Connoisseur's Complete Period Guides. The Regency* (*The Connoisseur*)
GEORGE, M. Dorothy, *London Life in the Eighteenth Century* (1925 – Peregrine Edition, 1966)
GRAHAM, J. T. *Weights and Measures* (Shire Publications, 1979)

HIBBERT, Christopher, *The English. A Social History* (Grafton, 1987)
HILL, Douglas, *A Hundred Years of Georgian London* (Macdonald, 1970)
HUGHES-HALLETT, Penelope, *Jane Austen. My Dear Cassandra*. (Collins and Brown, 1991)
JACKSON, Gordon, *Hull in the Eighteenth Century* (Oxford University Press, 1972)
KILVINGTON, Ben, *Ben Kilvington & Co.* (Sessions of York, 1989)
KNIGHT, Charles Brunton, *History of York* (Herald Printing Works, 1942)
LAW, Barrie, *York. A Time to Remember*
MALDEN, John, *Register of York Freemen 1680-1986* (Sessions of York, 1989)
MELL, George, *Writing Antiques* (Shire Publications, 1980)
MURRAY, Hugh, *Photographs and Photographers of York. The Early Years* (YA YAS and Sessions of York, 1986)
PITT-LENNOX, Lord William, *Coaching and Anecdotes of the Road* (Hurst and Blackett, 1876)
PUPILS OF THE JOSEPH ROWNTREE SCHOOL. *A View of the Shambles Past and Present*
RAFFALD, Elizabeth, *The Experienced English Housekeeper,* 1807 (Chester)
SCOTT, Sir Walter, *Ivanhoe* 1819
SESSIONS, W. K. & E. M., *Printing in York from the 1490s* (Sessions of York, 1976)
SESSIONS, W. K. & E. M., *The Tukes of York* (Sessions of York, 1971)
SESSIONS, William, *Sessions of York and their Printing Forebears* (1985)
SMITH, Graham, *King's Cutters. the Revenue Service and the War Against Smuggling* (Conway Maritime Press, 1983)
STURT, George, *The Wheelwright's Shop* (Cambridge University Press, 1948)
SUMMERSON, Sir John, *Georgian London* (Penguin Books, 1962)
TURNER, Thomas, *Diary of a Georgian Shopkeeper*
WALLROND, Sallie, *The Encyclopaedia of Driving* (*Country Life*)
WILLIS, Ronald, *Portrait of York* (Hale, 1972)
WOODFORDE, James, *The Diary of a Country Parson 1758-1802* (Oxford University Press)

Lease Registers of the Dean and Chapter of York
Poll List for 1818
The Cries of York for the Amusement of Good Children, 1811
York Chronicle, 1811-1820
York Courant, 1811-1820
York Herald, 1811-1820
York Trade Directories

Index

ACOMB, Joseph, 23
Alexander, Ann, 42-45 passim
Alexander, William, 41-45 passim
Allen, George, 27
Anley, William, 78
Aspinall, Mr, 51
Assembly Rooms, 8, 11, 31, 76
Astley, Mr, 77

BAKER, James, 69
Baker, William, 35, 36
Barber, James, 78, 79
Bartholoman, mr, 78
Bayldon & Berry, 38
Beal, George, 70
Beal, Thomas, 70
Bearpark, Mr, 21
Beckley, John, 38
Bell, David, 22
Bellerby, John, 73
Bickers & Sowerby, 32, 81
Blanchard, Mr, 52
Bootham, 17, 35, 62, 75
Bramley & Co, 56
Brearey & Morley, 27, 28
Breary & Myers, 28, 29
Bridge Street, 39, 67
Brocklebank, Joseph, 70
Brown, Mr, 15, 16
Brown, Richard, 37

CALVERT, Leonard, 26, 53, 54, 55

Calvert, Thomas, 55
Carey, John, 43, 44
Castlegate, 17, 35, 39-32 passim, 45, 56, 80
Catchasides, William, 27
Cattle, Robert, 78
Cattle & Barber, 77, 78, 79
Cautley, Mr, 69
Cave, Henry, 27, 35, 46, 53, 60, 62, 68
Cave, William, 46, 53, 63
Champlay, Mr, 67
Clark, George, 23
Clark, William, 23
Clementshaw, Mr, 4
Cloak, James, 70
Clough, Benjamin, 56-59 passim
Cochrane, Thomas, 55
Coffee Yard, 46, 52, 66
Colliergate, 21, 35
Coney Street, 3, 4, 7, 9, 12, 13, 16, 19, 21, 23, 27, 32, 35, 50, 55, 56, 60, 68, 70, 73, 77, 78, 81
Cook, Joseph, 50, 51
Cooke, Mr, 17
Cooke & Son, 21
Cooper, Mrs, 14, 15
Coppergate, 39
Coppergate Nook, 80
Cowley, Mr, 19
Creaser, John, 23
Creaser, Matthew, 23
Creasor, Isaiah, 78
Cressey, Thomas, 78

DANCER, Miss, 67, 68
Dale, George, 55
Dale, Richard, 55
Davygate, 27
Deighton (bokseller), 46
Dodgson, Mr, 70
Doeg, David, 70

ELLIOT, Mr, 37, 81
Ellis, Francis, 73
Ellis, William, 56, 57
Erskine, Mr, 4

FERRAND & Dodgson, 62
Fisher, Joseph, 27
Forbes, Frances, 67
Forbes, William, 67
Foster, Mr and Miss, 48
Fossgate, 4
Frankland, Mr, 4

GATENBY, Edward, 62
Gillygate, 45, 75
Goodramgate, 73
Gorwood, Benjamin, 21
Green, George, 62

JACKSON, Edward, 76, 77
Johnson, John, 80
Jubbergate, 7, 13, 74

KELSALL, Mrs, 17, 18
Kilvington, Charles, 22
King, Jane, 73
Kingan, Mr, 80
Knapton, Samuel, 3, 73
Knowles, Daniel, 19
Knowlson, Mr, 39

LINFOOT, Ralph, 62
Little Stonegate, 27, 28
Lord Mayor's Walk, 56
Low Ousegate, 4, 5, 6, 34, 35, 36, 39, 67, 69
Low Petergate, 4
Lyon, Mrs, 2, 16, 17, 18

MACLEAN, Mr, 56
McLean, Mr, 4
Mallatrat, Frederick, 60, 61
Marshall, Mrs, 73
Micklegate, 23, 26, 35, 39, 54, 73, 78, 81
Middleton, John, 71
Minster Gates, 45
Mnster Yard, 14, 32
Monkman, Mr, 39
Morgan, Mrs, 7, 50
Morley & Wales, 28
Mush, John, 74
Myers, Christopher, 28

NEW Street, 60, 77

OGLEFORTH, 27

PALMER (apothecary), 15, 46, 47, 65, 66, 68, 69
Pape, Mr, 39
Parsons & Blanchard, 4
Parsons, John, 8, 10, 11, 12, 13, 49, 51
Peacock, Mrs, 32, 33, 49, 50, 51
Peter Lane, 71, 74
Petergate, 52

Pickering, John, 45
Pomfret, William, 19, 20, 21
Poole, Mr, 24
Potter, John, 23
Potts, Mr, 80
Prests, 62, 69
Pulleyn, Robert, 51
Pullon, Thomas, 52, 79

RAIMES, Mr, 69
Rhodes, Mr, 59, 60
Ridley, Mrs, 56
Rusby, Hugh, 73

ST ANDREWGATE, 16
St Helen's Square, 12, 13, 24, 38, 45, 51, 59
St Sampson's Square, 35, 80
St Saviourgate, 35, 62, 70
Sanderson, Mr, 55
Scott, William, 55
Severs, Thomas, 35
Shambles, 6, 35
Sherwood, Lucy, 39
Sigsworth, David, 39
Smith, John, 35
Sollitt, William, 74
Spence, 46
Spencer, Francis, 13
Spurr, 23, 24
Spurr & Lockwood, 69
Spurriergate, 7, 21, 23, 32, 37, 38, 50, 52, 53, 62, 78, 81
Stephenson, Henry, 16
Stephenson, Mr, 32
Steventon & Bownas, 55

Stodhart, John, 21, 22
Stodhart, Thomas, 22
Stonegate, 3, 4, 15, 16, 17, 18 19, 19 20, 21, 22, 26, 27, 31, 46, 47, 52, 55, 70, 78
Storry, 46
Sutcliffe & Co, 66
Sweeting, Mr, 63
Swinegate, 73

TAYLOR, John, 74
Terry, Joseph, 38
Thursday Market, 35, 80
Todd's Bookshop, 15, 17, 18
Todd, John, 46
Trout, John, 55
Tuke, William, 41
Tuke, William, 41, 42

WALMGATE, 22, 43
Water Lane, 43
Watson, Hugh, 52
Watson, Mr, 78
Waud, Christopher, 13
Welbank, Mr, 18, 32
Westoby, Edward, 79
Whitewell, William, 79
Wiseman, Mr, 27
Wisker, J., 7
Wolstenholme, Dean, 74f
Wolstenholme, Francis, 45, 75
Wolstenholme, John, 45, 46, 67

PLAN of the City of YORK

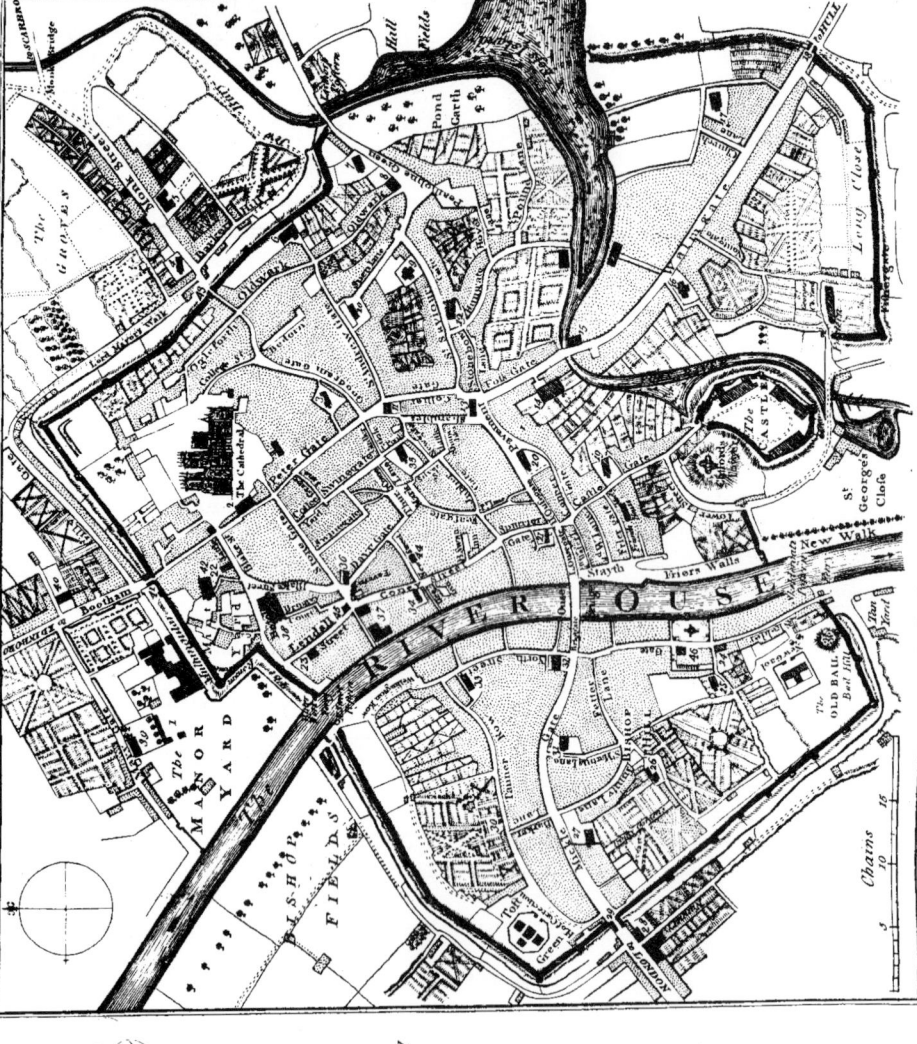

1 St Mary's Abbey
2 St Michael le Belfrey
3 Trinity Ch Goodramgate
4 St Maurice Monk Street
5 The County Hospital
6 Merchant Taylor's Hall
7 St Cuthbert's Peasholm Green
8 St Anthony's Hall or B. C. School
9 Unitarian Chapel
10 The Free School
11 Chryft Church
12 St Saviour's Ch
13 St Crux Ch
14 Merchant's Hall
15 Mr Wilson's Hospitals
16 St Dyon's Ch Walmgate
17 St Margaret's Ch
18 Walmgate Bar
19 St Mary's Caftlegate
20 All Saints Pavement
21 St Michael's Spurriergate
22 Roman Catholic Chapel
23 Independent Chapel
24 Mr Middleton's Hospital
25 St Mary Bishop Hill the Elder
26 St Mary Bishop Hill the Younger
27 Trinity Ch Mickelgate
28 St Thomas Hospital
29 Mickegate Bar
30 Lady Hewlay's Hospital
31 St Martin's Ch
32 St Johns
33 All Saints North Street
34 St Martin's Coney Street
35 St Sampson's Ch
36 St Helen's Church
37 Manfion Ho. & Guild Hall
38 The Afsembly Rooms